DATE DUE			
DEC 21 '9			
DEC 21 '9			
MAY 8 96			

EVE TEMPTED:

WRITING AND SEXUALITY IN HAWTHORNE'S FICTION

Eve Tempted
Writing and Sexuality in Hawthorne's Fiction
Allan Gardner Lloyd Smith

CROOM HELM
London & Sydney

BARNES AND NOBLE BOOKS
Totowa, New Jersey

©1984 A.G. Lloyd Smith
Croom Helm Ltd, Provident House, Burrell Row
Beckenham, Kent BR3 1AT
Croom Helm Australia Pty Ltd, First Floor, 139 King Street,
Sydney, NSW 2001, Australia

British Library Cataloguing in Publication Data

Lloyd Smith, A.G.
    Eve tempted.
    1. Hawthorne, Nathaniel—Criticism and
    interpretation
    I. Title
    813'.3   PS1888
    ISBN 0-7099-2368-6

First published in the USA 1983
Barnes & Noble Books
81 Adams Drive
Totowa, New Jersey, 07512

Library of Congress Cataloging in Publication Data

Lloyd Smith, Allan Gardner.
    Eve tempted.

    Bibliography: p.
    Includes index.
    1. Hawthorne, Nathaniel, 1804-1864—Criticism and inter-
pretation. 2. Sex in literature. 3. Hawthorne, Nathaniel,
1804-1864—Biography—Psychology. 4. Novelists,
American—19th century—Biography. I. Title.
PS1892.S47S6   1984   813'.3   84-3009
    ISBN 0-389-20486-2

Printed and bound in Great Britain

CONTENTS

INTRODUCTION

Hawthorne's historical situation as a writer of fiction in the first half of the nineteenth century has not always received the critical attention it requires. His education at Bowdoin College indoctrinated him according to the tenets of the Common Sense school, but his later proximity to the American Romantics, or Transcendentalists, in Salem and Concord offered a very different reading of "nature." The economic and social position of Hawthorne's mother and sisters, and later his own family, can best be described as marginal, a term which also serves to indicate his own intellectual and religious positions [1]. Hawthorne never seems to have accepted either of the major philosophical doctrines of his age, preferring instead to investigate the suppressed complexities that were elided in the opposing claims of Lockean and Kantian derivatives [2].

Amos Bronson Alcott, with his talent for revealing overstatement, as in his **Orphic Sayings** in **The Dial** (1840), shows the conflict in relief: "God, man, nature, are a divine synthesis, whose parts it is an impiety to sunder. Genius must preside devoutly over all investigations, or analysis, with her murderous knife, will seek impiously to probe the vitals of being" [3].On one side, the unity of man, God, and nature; on the other the "murderous knife" of analysis, represented, perhaps, by the counterthrusts of Princeton: "As there are certain limits to intellectual powers, which the immortal Locke endeavoured to ascertain, and beyond which we float in the region of midnight, so those who have forgotten these cautions have in their most original speculations only reproduced the delirium of other times, which in the cycle of opinion has come back upon us "like a phantasma or a hideous

1

dream" [4]. Hawthorne was closest to the new
transcendentalist opinions but, as a very near
neighbour, more concerned to challenge them. He
joined, and rather quickly left, the experimental
community at Brook Farm; he lived down the road
from Emerson in Concord, and wrote in the study of
the Old Manse, where Emerson had written "Nature"
in 1836: but what he wrote contradicted the sage;
he married Sophia Peabody, sister of the famous
Elizabeth (who kept school with Alcott and then ran
a bookshop in West Street, Boston, which became a
centre for radical reformers), but Hawthorne
resisted incorporation into the Peabody school of
spiritual improvement.

His resistance was worked out within the
intricacies of the discourse of "presence" of the
American Romantics. To understand this it is
necessary to return to the history of the episteme
of the early American nineteenth century. Locke had
been fully adopted by the American intellectual
establishment, because his ideas seemed uniquely
suitable for the national experience, without
posing any threat to religious doctrine [5]. But
the post-Lockean developments of his theory by
Berkeley, and by "materialists" such as Condillac,
or the "infidel" Hume, appeared to undermine some
certitudes. Berkeley's elaboration of the gulf
between perception and object, which priviliged
perception over the reality of phenomena posed one
sort of epistemological difficulty; sceptical and
materialist versions of the senses and behaviour
posed another. Perhaps the objective world did not
exist: a notion anethematic to empiricist thinkers;
but perhaps (what was even worse,) only the
objective world existed, without any spiritual
sanction. Since both propositions were intolerable
to right minded Bible readers the middle path
advocated by Thomas Reid, Dugald Stewart, and
Thomas Brown as "common sense," quickly dominated
the American philosophy. This theory held that
conviction of right and wrong existed within the
mind as an inherent moral sense; and that there
could be no doubt of the existence of the external
world, which was perceived immediately, not
indirectly. Doubters were invited to test other
notions against the universal experience of mankind
[6]. Hawthorne was taught moral philosophy at
Bowdoin by one of the principal American exponents
of the common sense school, Thomas Upham.

But the calm invincibility of these doctrines
in America, together with their consequences in
2

Introduction

religion: rationality rather than enthusiasm; a
stress on conscience; a scepticism regarding
miracles, or the need for miraculous evidences; led
to a reaction against them which phrased itself in
terms of presence, fulness, immediacy. Emerson was
one of those Unitarians who felt the need for
inspiration rather than rational persuasion, belief
rather than quiet conviction, and he, like Alcott,
Jones Very, Theodore Parker, and George Ripley,
found in transcendental philosophy (a somewhat
speculative outgrowth of Kant's arguments,) a new
set of legitimations to oppose to the Scots.

The transcendentalists argued that calculating
philosophies were unworthy of the godlike powers in
man, who had access to divine intuition: an
immediate knowledge not only of the things of the
external world but of their essence, their place in
a greater scheme. This, in a sense, stepped behind
the common sense assertion of immediate sense
perception of the phenomenal world: by asserting
knowledge of the "noumenal" it offered a superior
immediacy, and gave the self a fuller "presence."
By asserting the unity of all things the
transcendentalists were able to insist on living
spirit rather than dead matter, and neo-Platonic
rather than Newtonian understandings of force and
mass, with the hope of a deep integration between
all apparent separations: "Love and gravity are a
twofold action of one life," Bronson Alcott
claimed. The ideal, then, must be to become closer
to the source. As George Ripley expressed it, "The
visible universe is to us what our invisible souls
choose to make it," therefore we should make things
which are unseen the chief object of attention. "In
so doing, we become conversant with the primal
source of reality. We ascend to the original
fountain of Being, from which the streams that flow
forth receive their properties and their
direction..." [7]. If some of this imagery holds a
sexual implication, that is not fortuitous: the
goal of personal integration at such levels of
intensity must engage with feelings that are
charged with sexual experience, as is the case in
religious enthusiasm generally [8]. But if the self
could ascend to full presence, it could equally be
vulnerable to absence. Margaret Fuller, who
Hawthorne sometimes met at Concord as well as at
Brook Farm, spoke for all her companions when she
said: "The heart which hopes and dares is also
accessible to terror, and this falls upon it like a
thunderbolt. It can never defend itself at the

3

moment, it is so surprised" [9].

Presence, then, and the terror that might be felt when the heart hoped and dared to open itself to the ultimate, became the terms of discourse in the transcendental group. Presence inspired the questions: what is original action? What is the self that must be trusted? "Who is the Trustee?" as Emerson asked in "Self-Reliance," assuring his listeners that "the magnetism which all original action exerts is explained when we inquire the reason of self-trust." Spontaneity; instinct; intuition; was his answer: "In that deep force, the last fact behind which analysis cannot go, all things find their common origin" [10].

Hawthorne felt some sympathy with these doctrines: valorising the "heart," asking for reverence in investigations of it, giving priority to intuition and instinct over reason and analysis, and maintaining a sense of divine purposes behind human events. But as if fated with a sort of Midas touch (a king for whom he seems to have felt some sympathy, given his treatment of the story in **A Wonder Book**), Hawthorne's best efforts to be a transcendentalist produced not an enthusiastic uplift but demoralisation, as the most cherished concepts: "heart," "love," "beauty," "Eden," "nature," "innocence," "speech," turned to mineral when he examined them. Even more tempting as an analogy is the Medusa gaze, which turns its objects to stone, because the petrifications to which life seemed always susceptible are what he registered most definitively whenever he looked into the sources of human behaviour. Distance, deferral, spacing, the supplement, are some of the terms that have come to seem applicable to Hawthorne's displacements, particularly as these have been articulated by Jacques Derrida in his work on Rousseau [11]. "Writing" thereby becomes a meta-term, describing the aspects of "presence" that mean it is not immediate and originary. As is true of Rousseau, Hawthorne's suspicions of writing were matched by his sense of the involvement of writing within speech, however innocently natural or unmediated it might at first appear; and the involvement of "writing" (in the sense of distance, deferral, the supplement), even within perception or feeling itself.

Hawthorne's interest in the process by which the living becomes inanimate, or conversely, the inanimate seems to live; and his sense of the hardening of the fleeting instant as it becomes the

4

past, before it can even be known; determines the shape of many of his characteristic fantasies, and sometimes even distorts the form of his novels. "Trace" becomes an obsessive motif which, in **The House of the Seven Gables** and **The Marble Faun** almost obscures the diegesis. In the late romances plot collapsed under the weight of the "Bloody Footstep" and the "Bloody Flower," the sanguinea sanguinissima. But my argument will be that the occasional confusions and infelicities of his projects provide hinge-terms enabling us to see how seriously he pursued the issues of authenticity, sincerity and presence, against the background of their naively confident assertion by the transcendentalists. The point of brisure, perhaps predictably, is provided by sexuality, in its rather specific manifestations around the half-century, which interwove sexual content in all occulted contexts. Hence the twin focuses of this book: supplementarity and the history of sexuality, which between them provide not a key for the unlocking of mystery, but the means of furthering our investigations of Hawthorne beyond the blank wall, the reified "heart," before which criticism has absent mindedly paused.

I propose not to deal with the historical Hawthorne, an elusive and unknowable figure at this depth of analysis, but rather with the various "Hawthornes" discoverable in the texts, producing, in so far as my method might be described as psycho-biographical, a fragmented biography of the writer posited by the material. This allows for a criticism that probes deeply into areas explored in the past through psychoanalytic studies, but without encountering the objections levelled at such approaches. These objections include the impossibility of conducting a full analysis on the basis of such limited material and without the interaction of analyst with analysand; the imperialism of psychoanalytic doctrines, as in Frederick Crew's study of Hawthorne, **The Sins of the Fathers** [12], and above all, the question of intentionality, for the work of criticism is to illuminate the texts, not to invent an historical figure with which it can explain them away as the products of neurosis. My method is based largely on the theries of Wolfgang Iser, who retrieves from the text both an implied author and an implied reader, brought into being during the act of reading [13]. An advantage of this perspective is that it provokes attention to the culture of the

"author" within which the codes for the production
of meaning are inscribed, away from a reductive
insistence upon overdetermination by personal
experience: towards, for example, Shelley's **The
Cenci**, or Guido Reni's painting of Beatrice Cenci;
away from a supposed disposition towards incest in
the Hawthorne or Manning families. But above all I
hope to stimulate a new kind of reading of
Hawthorne, which desacralises the texts while
reclaiming some of their lost significances.

NOTES

1. Hawthorne's economic and social marginality
is described in Arlin Turner's biography: **Nathaniel
Hawthorne** (New York: Oxford University Press,
1980), and Robert Cantwell, **Nathaniel Hawthorne,
The American Years** (New York: Rinehart & Co, 1948).
    2. An account of the opposing philosophical
systems is J.W. Fay's **American Psychology Before
William James** (New York: Octagon Press, 1966).
    3. Amos Bronson Alcott in **The Dial**, July,
1840, I, pp. 85-98.
    4. J.W. Alexander, Albert Dod, Charles Hodge,
"Transcendentalism of the Germans and of Cousin and
its Influence on Opinion in this Country." **The
Biblical Repository and Princeton Review** Jan 1839,
in Perry Miller, ed, **The Transcendentalists**
(Cambridge, Mass: Harvard University Press, 1971).
    5. Merle Curti, "The Great Mr. Locke,
America's Philosopher 1783-1861," **Huntington
Library Bulletin** XL (April 1937) pp.111-113.
    6. See, for example, G. Stanley Hall, "On the
History of American College Text-Books," **American
Antiquarian Society** (April 1894) pp. 137-174.
    7. George Ripley, "Discourses on the
Philosophy of Religion" (Boston, 1836), in Miller,
op cit. Ripley was the moving spirit of Brook Farm,
a close associate of Hawthorne for a time.
    8. William James noticed this aspect of
religious mania. See **The Varieties of Religious
Experience** (Glasgow: Collins Fountain Books, 1977)
p.398.
    9. Margaret Fuller, Journal, 25th November,
1843, in **Memoirs of Margaret Fuller** (Boston, 1852).
    10. "Self-Reliance" in **R.W. Emerson, Selected
Prose and Poetry**, ed R.L. Cook (New York: Holt
Rinehart and Winston, 1969) p. 81.
6

11. Jacques Derrida, **Of Grammatology** tr. G.C. Spivak (Baltimore: Johns Hopkins University Press, 1974).
12. Frederick Crews, **The Sins of the Fathers** (New York: Oxford University Press, 1966).
13. Wolfgang Iser, **The Act Of Reading** (London: Routledge & Kegan Paul, 1978).

1 THE ELABORATED SIGN OF THE SCARLET LETTER

A curious feature of American romantic writing is the choice of a culturally established sign or emblem as the basis for thematic elaboration and symbolic extension. Examples include Melville's use of the doubloon in **Moby-Dick**, or the oval stern piece in "Benito Cereno"; Poe's recourse to alchemical texts and legends in "The Fall of the House of Usher" and the word "discovery" in "MS.Found in a Bottle": the list could be greatly extended but the outstanding instance is **The Scarlet Letter**. The letter exists as a double sign before Hawthorne embroiders it: firstly it is an alphabetic sign, the initial letter and to some extent therefore standing for alphabeticism, language, or more specifically, writing; and secondly it is an historically determined signifier of proscribed behaviour, the meaning it contains when worn on the breast being "adulteress". Perhaps there is a third signifying function: the letter is "discovered" by Hawthorne as a token of the truth of Surveyer Pue's story and an evidence of the existence of the past in the present. A peculiarity of the alphabetic sign, even the essence of it, is that it does not uniquely represent anything except a sound, it is empty of content and therefore free to take on any meaning required of it in the formation of words [1]. The scarlet letter is precise in its signifying of adultery, yet it retains an openness deriving from alphabeticity and may come to stand for able, or even angel. In these aspects of preexistence and hermeneutic complexity the elaborated sign resembles allegory: the allegorical pretext is already established and "given", yet its

9

modification in achieving a particular form opens
the possibility of alternative meanings according
to the level of exegesis. In its manifestation as
object, or rag of cloth [2], however, the letter
resembles those gothic signifiers, guilty documents
or bloodstained marks, which insist upon a
predetermined response in the audience or
readership, and it thereby draws our attention to
the semiology of association theory in Hawthorne's
period [3]. Consideration of the letter as an
elaborated sign, then, suggests three areas of
interrelated concern: the question of writing
(especially as the shadow of the spoken or
unspoken); the use of allegory and typology; and
the aesthetics of preordained response.

Hester's punishment is that she should be
written on and be unable to efface the inscription.
The sentence of the magistrates suggests that their
community is especially distinguished by a
preoccupation with the status of the written and
that this preoccupation may take curious forms
outside of the usual domain of writing. An example
of such extension is to be found at the
institutional centre of the community, on the walls
of the Governor's mansion, which are "decorated
with strange and seemingly cabalistic figures and
diagrams, suitable to the quaint taste of the
[previous] age, which had been drawn in the stucco
when newly laid on, and had now grown hard and
durable, for the admiration of after times"(I,103).
The passage proposes that the customs and values of
an earlier age have become mechanical and hardened
into a structure which oppresses its inheritors, in
part, perhaps, because of their inability to
understand them. There is here too a suggestion
that the old Puritan faith brought more with it
across the Atlantic in the form of superstition and
occult ritual than its adherents may have overtly
acknowledged. Both of these propositions are
significant in understanding **The Scarlet Letter**.
But the mode of the persistence of the past in the
present is inscription in the guise of "decoration"
in an inappropriate place: language in its written
form has spread over the surface of the artifacts
of the colony [4]. An implication of this may be
that nothing manmade is "blank" however difficult
it may be to decipher its meaning. The bright, rich
embroidery favoured by the more powerful members of
Boston holds similar implications, especially as
Hester's needlework spreads the embroidery of the
Scarlet Letter throughout the settlement: her work
10

is seen on the ruff of the Governor, worn by
military men on their scarfs and the minister on
his band; it decorates the baby's cap and is shut
up to moulder away in coffins; but it never appears
on the veils of brides (I,83), an omission which
serves to stress the associations implicit in its
other uses. Written on herself, Hester then writes
on the community in "manifold emblematic devices"
(I,82), and the message that she writes is the
message of her own exegesis of the letter, a
luxuriant exfoliation as subversive of the colony's
official statutes as it is of the bare outline of
the typographic sign "A".

The alphabetical sign itself proliferates in a
sort of printing which fulfills its essential
nature: reduplication. The red 'A' appears on
Dimmesdale's chest (or may do so); on Pearl, and in
Pearl, since she is another version of the letter;
and in the sky as a gigantic letter made by a
comet. It appears, hugely magnified, in the convex
mirror of the Governor (I,106); is engraved on
Hester's tombstone; survives as a rag of cloth; and
finally leaves its "deep print" in the author's
brain, "where long meditation has fixed it in very
undesirable distinctness" (I,259). In its
manifestations as portent the letter is structured
as typology; as personal inscription it describes
a psychology of obsessional identity and symbolic
preception; and as epitaph it assumes a heraldic
function as the arms of the new world. Finally, as
a haunting imprint the letter has anagogical
qualities, expressed in Hawthorne's description of
its mystical meaning, subtly communicated to his
sensibilities but evading analysis by his mind,
streaming forth from the letter like a sensation of
burning heat. In a sense all these meanings are
embroidery, since any particular meaning ascribed
to the outline is only a single version of an
infinite potentiality which is ultimately
blankness. Because the alphabetical sign can mean
anything, it must itself mean nothing. Yet in its
irreducible existence as sign, the letter stands as
a model for Hawthorne's relationship to the past:
the past intransigently existing in the present and
offering a plethora of possible interpretations for
the perceiving consciousness, perhaps requiring a
sort of embroidery to bring it to life, but
occulted behind any particular reading of it.

The Scarlet Letter is saturated in typological
reference and although this is appropriate in an
historical novel set in Puritan times Hawthorne's

11

use of the convention is more than an adoption of
historical dress. The Puritans saw every earthly
phenomenon as a potential message from God, or, as
Ursula Brumm expresses it, "potentially a sign used
by God to proclaim His will like an inlaid motto to
mankind" [5]. The ambiguity inherent in the
interpretation of such signs is exploited in
Dimmesdale's egotistical reading of the "awful
hieroglyphics" in which the firmament itself
appears as "no more than a fitting page for his
soul's history and fate," a reading which is
confirmed by the vision of other witnesses but
denied by their alternative interpretations of the
message. Religious typology consists of the
interpretation of events as prefiguration, in the
way that the Old Testament could be seen to
prefigure the events of the New Testament [6]. But
in the practise of the American Puritans typology
became a means of interpreting the events of their
own experience in the new world as revelations:
"Nothing was more common, in those days, than to
interpret all meteoric appearances, and other
natural phenomena, that occurred with less
regularity than the rise and set of sun and moon,
as so many revelations from a supernatural source.
Thus, a blazing spear, a sword figures Indian
warfare. Pestilence was known to have been
foreboded by a shower of crimson light" (I,154).
The inevitable tendency was that every visible
object should become "a potential emblem, behind
which an ever paler God stands in an ever more
puzzling relationship" [7].

The confusion elicited by the celestial letter
"A" is reiterated in the versions of Hester's
letter and Hester herself as a "type" of shame
(I,79), or as "Able" (I,161). The sign has multiple
meanings, which do not coalesce as "symbol" but
remain antagonistic to one another [8]. This is
what is inherent in Hawthorne's sceptical attitude
towards any supposedly certain knowledge, indeed
his hostility towards the written itself, whether
law, exclusive exegesis or insistent identification
of personality; even the certainties implied by
literary construction which he so persistently
undermines by positing alternatives and by
disavowing the authoritative position of the
writer. Karl Keller sees Hawthorne as one of a
group disaffected from "plebeian typology," that
is, a typology freed from its biblical anchorage,
and a structure of thought rather than an
eschatology. "Plebeian allegorising," which Keller
12

considers the principal nineteenth century mode,
"begins with a fact of one's life or a feature of
nature and locates the divine behind it after the
formula a=B if B>a: a metaphor elevated to cosmic
symbolism" [9]. Ambiguity is a way of resisting the
imperialism of such readings, offering "not a
desperately divided state of mind or tormented
perspective, not mere conflict, but balance without
resolution, without coherence - a condition that
would undercut any proposed antitype" [10]. Whereas
Emersonian nature is transparent, a set of types,
Hawthorne's generates opposing typological
readings, all of which are questioned in the text.
Still, Hawthorne's response as he confronts the
letter is in some respects a secular version of
typological practise: he considers it as an
exceptional object carrying a significant message
which must be interpreted to the community (for
which it may be prophetic in the sense that it
explains the community to itself, or in the sense
that typology offers the possibility of a
reapprehension of the past in view of its
prefigurative aspect), with the aid of the scroll
enwrapping it; Mr Surveyer Pue's document.

As Hester wears the letter on her breast she
becomes the letter and, in the eyes of her
community, nothing else: she appears only as whore,
the word spoken even by those who do not know its
meaning, "a word that had no distinct import to
[the children's] own minds, but was none the less
terrible to her, as proceeding from lips that
babbled it unconsciously" (I,185). Such a reduction
of personal identity to one constituent is also
manifested in the distorting reflection seen in
Governor Bellingham's armour (I,106), another
exaggeration of one single feature until it
obliterates the woman behind it and her complex
history becomes reducible to a letter. But it is
not only the public view of Hester that is
dramatised here; it is her own view, as we register
from the fact that this is a mirror image in the
polished armour. Her public branding has been the
"great and marked event" which gives the colour to
her lifetime, "as if a new birth, with stronger
assimilations than the first, had converted the
forest land ... into Hester Prynne's wild and
dreary, but life-long home" (I,80). Thus Hester
accepts the radical simplification of her identity
as "the type of shame" (I,79), much as Roderick
Elliston adopts the serpent as his own essence:
"the fouler the crime, with so much the more

13

difficulty does the perpetrator prevent it from thrusting up its snake-like head to frighten the world; for it is that cancer, or that crime, which constitutes their respective individuality" (X,273). Similarly, once the "language" is known, others can read it: Chillingworth seeks the letter elsewhere, and discovers it articulating itself on Dimmesdale. My stress on morbid pathologies of identity reflects Hawthorne's own critique of the perverse substitutions involved in such self-identifications, and implicit in the written (as opposed to spoken) passion such phenomena exhibit. The ultimate case of imprinting of the letter, of course, is little Pearl, who is "the scarlet letter in another form; the scarlet letter endowed with life!" (I,102,207). In Pearl the letter has achieved an hereditary embodiment; the environmental adaptation has become written into the genetic code. This is potentially the most extreme perversion, in keeping with which the narrative offers frequent suggestions of demonic intrusion in her making. Pearl has to be redeemed in the course of the novel, or rather, she has to be humanized, in a movement which illustrates Hawthorne's solution to the problem of proliferating substitution.

Apart from the obvious similitude of her dress and appearance, Pearl is shown to have a deep identification with the scarlet letter: it is the first object she sees with any conscious vision (I,96), and it elicits a curious smile and "odd expression of the eyes" from her whenever her gaze fixes upon it, "like the stroke of sudden death" (I,97). She behaves as though "the only thing for which she had been sent into the world was to make out its hidden import," when she fashions her own version of the emblem out of eel-grass (I,178). This apparent naturalizing of the letter, replacing its hellfired scarlet with a fresh green, might seem to suggest the redemptive power of Pearl's innocence, were it not for the choice of "eel-grass" with which to construct the replica, which only replaces one sign of the Satanic with another. It would be curious too, if an episode immediately following Hester's meeting with Chillingworth on the beach should be chosen for a heavenly revelation. Hester's temporising reply to Pearl's insistent questioning: "And as for the scarlet letter, I wear it for the sake of its gold thread," described by Hawthorne as the first time she had been false to the symbol on her bosom

14

(I,181), is more fully in accordance with the implications of this meeting. But in a sense her reply is more honest than she supposes, because the "gold thread" of the letter is her own embroidery of it, and that is indeed why she continues to wear it, if embroidery is understood as the creation of a transfiguring personal meaning out of the bare sign. The possibility that Pearl's "inevitable tendency to hover about the enigma of the scarlet letter" like an inner quality of her being," or an "appointed mission" (I,180), might be providential is raised by her new appearance of sympathetic earnestness but at once belied by the direction of her question "why does the minister keep his hand over his heart?" and by the mischievous look which soon follows (I,181). The occasion of Pearl's liberation from the thrall of the letter as identity is the same as Dimmesdale's, Hester's, and Chillingworth's: the public <u>speaking</u> of the truth that has formerly been <u>written</u> humanises her and breaks the spell of the letter, her errand as a "messenger of anguish" now fulfilled (I,256). By his determination to "speak out the whole" Dimmesdale is able to overcome the ever-receding vista of secondariness inflected by the letter and re-engage with immediacy, as in his kissing Pearl, thus subduing not only Hester's letter, and the one on his own breast, but also the essential principle of the letter within himself: "He bids you look again at Hester's scarlet letter! He tells you that, with all its mysterious horror, it is but the shadow of what he bears on his breast, and even this, his own red stigma, is no more than the type of what has seared his inmost heart!" (I,255) But it is now necessary to develop the full extent of what is entailed in the idea of the written and the spoken; an issue of crucial importance for Hawthorne and other Romantic authors of his period.

Dimmesdale's description of the letter as but the shadow of his physical stigma, and that only a type of the original, which has seared his heart, will serve as a starting point because it demonstrates the idea of a series of substitutions, at the end of which appears the written sign. From the essential truth within the heart; to an expressive gesture (the stigma); then to a formal written sign, is an hierarchical series in which "something else" is substituted for the higher reality. A missing term in Dimmesdale's sequence is the articulation of speech, which logically (and in the models available to Hawthorne) precedes writing while succeeding the integrity of the mute gesture. It will be useful henceforth to refer to Jacques Derrida's analysis of Rousseau's **Essay on the Origin of Language** [11] (albeit without insisting that Hawthorne followed Rousseau's argument precisely, although he did read extensively in the **Oeuvres Completes** in the 1830's and again in June and July 1848 [12],) since Rousseau and Hawthorne appear to share certain cardinal assumptions which bear directly on **The Scarlet Letter**.

Rousseau fixes the distinction between speech and personal gesture (immediate sign) by stressing the priority of presence:

> Although the language of gesture and spoken language are equally natural, still the first is easier and depends less upon conventions. For more things affect our eyes than our ears. Also, visual forms are more varied than sounds, and more expressive, saying more in less time. Love, it is said, was the inventor of drawing. It might also have invented speech, though less happily. Not being very well pleased with it, it disdains it; it has livelier ways of expressing itself. How could she say things to her beloved, who traced his shadow with such pleasure. What sounds might she use to render this movement of the magic wand (**Essay**, p.6).

Gesture is close to the immediacy of touch, although a certain small distance is implicit within it [13], speech represents a further stage of distantiation, writing yet a further, and the single alphabetic sign (which cannot in this case be spoken), is a step further again. Speech, although one stage more removed from the "presence" of the self than gesture, nevertheless has the feature of penetration. Rousseau claims, "the passions have their gestures, but they also have their accents, and these accents, which thrill us, these tones of voice that cannot fail to be heard, penetrate to the very depths of the heart, carrying there the emotions they wring from us, forcing us in spite of ourselves to feel what we hear (**Essay**, pp.8,9). This may be compared to Hawthorne's account of the power of Dimmesdale's voice (I,142). Despite the reservation implied by "forcing us in spite of ourselves" and similarly inherent in the deceit of Dimmesdale's tones of pathos, speech in this essentialist metaphysic is
16

spontaneous, primary, less remote from nature and truth than the petrifications of written language. Because "languages are made to be spoken, writing is nothing but a supplement of speech ..., speech represents thought through conventional signs, and writing represents speech in the same way; thus the art of writing is nothing but a mediated representation of thought..." (Rousseau, **Fragment on Pronunciation**). Rousseau situates the written at two removes from thought, as supplementary and substitutive, and there is ample evidence in **The Scarlet Letter** to suggest that Hawthorne does the same.

Dimmesdale's "Election Day" sermon provides a heavily mediated version of his inner experience: it is written during a fit of inspiration after the meeting with Hester in the forest and immediately following his temptations to blasphemy and corruption on the way home. He "fancied himself inspired; and only wondered that Heaven should see fit to transmit the grand and solemn music of its oracles through so foul an organ pipe as he" (I,225). This metaphor of man as an organ pipe for Heaven is an ironic echo of Emerson's doctrine that men rest like fountain-pipes on an unfathomed sea of thought and virtue [14]; and the subject of the sermon, "the relation between the Deity and the communities of mankind, with a special reference to the New England that they were here planting in the wilderness" (I,249), is the typological doctrine so effectively discomfited by Hawthorne's illustration of the meteor.

Never far from the narrative is the notion of signing one's name in the Black Book (I,117), that is, the act of writing as a consignment of the identity to an indissoluble contract with the devil, which is endemic in the Puritan community and typified in Mistress Hibbins, Governor Bellingham's sister. Hester also would have been tempted to sign that contract if Pearl were taken from her. She tells Pearl that she did once meet the Black Man, and the letter is his mark (I,185), a recognition of the magistrates' fanatical logocentrism which is also apparent in their inability to see Hester as anything but the substitute, that is, the Letter. The letter is a mark of <u>dis</u>-grace, the devil's mirror image of the Covenant, as the "Black Book" mirrors the Bible.

Hester uses the letter as a mask. Like Poe's "purloined letter" it is thrust forward in order to conceal the truth: her carefully chosen gray
17

garments make her "fade personally out of sight and outline," but the scarlet letter "brought her back from this twilight indistinctness, and revealed her under the moral aspect of its own illumination" (I,226), [15]. The "marble quietude" of her face is like the "frozen calmness of a dead woman's features" (I,226); and so we have the spectacle of an invisible or "dead" woman, whose label of "adulteress" paradoxically guarantees that she is proof against all scandal (I,234). Underneath the proclamation of her sin, which induces a negative hallucination of purity, she is thus able to conceal her essence, which remains "adulteress." For her "sin" is repeated when she meets Dimmesdale in the forest, although this time the action itself is elided, remaining only as literary trace in the description of the "natural" surroundings. The insistent topography of the forest meeting place is itself a memory of their sexual passion: the remains of a tall pine, now only a luxuriant heap of moss, provides a seat in a little dell with a brook flowing through the midst (I,186). Only a sexual interpretation can account for the insistence with which Hawthorne describes the brook as babbling a dark secret, and with which he returns over and over to the triptych's features of trees, dell and brook: "a secret dell, by a mossy tree-trunk, and near a melancholy brook" (I,217), or: the "little dell of solitude, and love, and anguish, and the mossy tree-trunk, where, sitting hand in hand, they had mingled their sad and passionate talk with the melancholy murmur of the brook" (I,239). This scene is a writing in natural signs of their sexual union (Melville's "Tartarus of Maids" holds a similar secret allegory), or rather it is both a writing and a re-writing in that the tree, once phallic, is now a mossy ruin (Dimmesdale's unmanned self), the dell is of "love" but now also of "solitude" and anguish" (Hester's sexual shame) and the brook, which was allegorically their sexual intermingling, is now identified with Pearl. Thus the deep pools, eddies and black depths of the stream (I,186), represent the guilt and mystery of her making, whereas its swifter and livelier passages reflect the vivacity of her individual identity. This provides an essential context for Pearl's reflection in the water of the stream; the suggestion that it might "mirror its revelations on the smooth surface of a pool" (I,186) that is, write the story of the adultery on a natural page; and Dimmesdale's
18

fantasy that the brook is "the boundary between two
worlds" and that Hester can never meet her Pearl
again (I,208). John T. Irwin sees Pearl's
reluctance to return to her mother in the forest
scene as due to her recognition of her own origin
in their union: "to Pearl the sight of Hester and
Dimmesdale together in the forest, each
transfigured by the rebirth of physical love, is
like a primal scene (consider the sexual overtones
of the remark 'another inmate had been admitted
within the circle of the mother's feelings'), a
child's glimpse of the ground from which it
originated" [16]. But beyond the psychological
realism of her response Pearl's dramatic part in
this scene is to substitute herself for her own
making in a reenactment of which the terms are
almost the same and yet crucially different, as in
the three scaffold scenes in which the integers of
Hester, Pearl and Dimmesdale are successively
recombined.
    The "natural signs" of Hawthorne's writing are
registrations of human events, not hieroglyphic
messages from God; deciphered they offer not
revelation but evidence of the human past.
Chillingworth is distorted by his evil passion
until his viciousness is written on his face, as
Dimmesdale's guilt is upon his breast and Hester
and Dimmesdale's adultery upon the forest.
Hawthorne's mistrust of nature as authentic
testimony for God appears in his even-handed
description of the sympathy of Nature as "that
wild, heathen Nature of the forest, never
subjugated by human law, nor illumined by higher
truth" (I,203). The forest is, however, at least
not unnatural like the laws of men; it sympathises
with Hester and Dimmesdale, and provides playmates
for the child who is shunned by her Puritan peers.
Unredeemed, and without revelatory powers, the
natural nevertheless provides a model for a "new
truth" which may one day "establish the whole
relation between man and woman on a surer ground of
mutual happiness" (I,263).
    Derrida's version of Rousseau again provides a
suggestive commentary on the issues involved here:

    Natural pity, which is illustrated
    archetypically by the relationship between
    mother and child, and generally by the
    relationship between life and death, commands
    like a gentle voice. In the metaphor of that
    soft voice the presence of the mother as well

as of Nature is at once brought in. That the
soft voice must be the mother's as well as
Nature's is clear from the fact that it is,
as the metaphor of the voice clearly always
indicates in Rousseau, a law. "No one is
tempted to disobey it" at the same time
because it is soft and because, being natural
and absolutely original, it is also
inexorable. That maternal law is a voice. Pity
is a voice. As opposed to writing, which is
without pity, the voice is always, in its
essence, the passage of virtue and good
passion. The order of pity "takes the place of
law," it supplements law, that is to say
instituted law.... One might say then that the
natural law, the gentle voice of pity, is not
only uttered by a maternal solicitude, it is
inscribed in our hearts by God. It concerns
the natural writing, the writing of the heart,
which Rousseau opposes to the writing of
reason. Only the latter is without pity, it
alone transgresses the interdict that, under
the name of natural affection, links the child
to the mother and protects life from death
[17].

The intertwining of natural and institutional law,
proposed as reciprocal supplements of one another,
precisely defines Hawthorne's area of concern, and
the metaphor of the gentle voice of natural pity,
illuminates the whole matter of voice versus
writing in **The Scarlet Letter**. The brook, babbling
sadly of mysteries past and future is exactly that
gentle voice of natural pity in opposition to the
legalistic severity with which the Puritans
pitilessly write their definition on Hester and
would even separate mother and child, seeing her as
a "type of her of Babylon" (I,110), [18]. The idea
of a "natural writing" inscribed upon our hearts by
God has its complement, in Derrida's view, in an
element of writing within speech itself, a
supplementarity that exists in the very nature of
language: "The ethic of the living word would be
perfectly respectable... if it did not live on a
delusion and a nonrespect for its own condition of
origin, if it did not dream in speech of a presence
denied to writing, denied by writing" [19]. The
element of writing within a speech "believed to be
transparent and innocent" [20], made Hawthorne,
more than Rousseau, suspicious, and severely
modifies the authenticity of the spoken word in **The**

The Elaborated Sign

Scarlet Letter whether uttered by hero and heroine
or by their Puritan antagonists.

The catechism demonstrates how Puritan written
law permeates even the spoken realm, for Pearl is
immediately identified by the Reverend Wilson with
the "pearl of great price" [Matthew xiii, 45-6],
and interrogated according to the verbal formula,
"who made thee?" (I,111). Her answer, that she was
plucked off the bush of wild roses beside the
prison, opposes a natural imaginative truth to the
formal enquiry but merely provokes a further series
of institutional categories; "without question, she
is equally in the dark as to her soul, its present
depravity, and future destiny" (I,112). Such
tendencies to writing within speech are also
satirised in the language given to the Puritan
children when they see Hester and Pearl and cry:
"Behold, verily, there is the woman of the scarlet
letter; and, of a truth, moreover, there is the
likeness of the scarlet letter running along by her
side! Come, therefore, and let us fling mud at
them!" (I,102) But it should not be assumed that a
more immediate and authentic speech is readily
available to Hester, Pearl, or Dimmesdale. Rather,
as Millicent Bell notes in her article "The
Obliquity of Signs," silence and inarticulateness
are here the condition of truth: Dimmesdale's
election sermon "is best understood when, in fact,
its words are indistinguishable and only the
mournful tone of his voice conveys his state to
Hester as she stands outside. Language, by
implication, misleads us, tells us nothing of the
heart, which has no language. Dimmesdale's
unintelligible murmur is like Pearl's babble or
the gibberish she speaks in his ear in the night
scaffold scene - perhaps a sacred speaking in
tongues, perhaps the non-sense of a messageless
world" [21]. This is only partly the case, however,
because the novel does include passages of true
speech - as in Hester's moving defence of her right
to keep Pearl, and Dimmesdale's final ability to
"speak out the whole" that is, speak the letter,
the apparently unutterable written sign, by his
confession and display of the letter as expressive
gesture, the word made flesh. Hawthorne in fact
maintains a balance and a reserve in establishing
the dominions of the spoken and the written, for
the two powerful spoken appeals just mentioned are
countervailed by a mistrust of speech at the heart
of the book and a victory for the written in its
conclusion. Hester's impassioned defence of a

21

mother's right to her child is allowed full
legitimacy by the author; but not so her equally
impassioned plea to Dimmesdale in the forest. Close
examination of this crucial passage shows that
Hester's argument is inflated by a rhetoric of
transcendentalism and moral perfectibility worthy
of a Mr Smooth-it-away [22]:

> "Thou art crushed under this seven years'
> weight of misery," replied Hester, fervently
> resolved to buoy him up with her own energy.
> "But thou shalt leave it all behind thee! It
> shall not cumber thy steps, as thou treadest
> along the forest-path; neither shalt thou
> freight the ship with it, if thou prefer to
> cross the sea. Leave this wreck and ruin here
> where it hath happened! Meddle no more with
> it! Begin all anew! Hast thou exhausted
> possibility in the failure of this one trial!
> Not so! The future is yet full of trial and
> success. There is happiness to be enjoyed!
> There is good to be done! Exchange this false
> life of thine for a true one. Be, if thy
> spirit summon thee to such a mission, the
> teacher and apostle of the red man. Or, - as
> is more thy nature, - be a scholar and a sage
> among the wisest and most renowned of the
> cultivated world. Preach! Write! Act! Do
> anything, save to lie down and die! Give up
> this name of Arthur Dimmesdale, and make
> thyself another, and a high one, such as thou
> canst wear without fear or shame. Why shouldst
> thou tarry so much as one other day in the
> torments that have so gnawed into thy life! -
> that have made thee feeble to will and to do!
> - that will leave thee powerless even to
> repent! Up, and away!" (I,198).

Hawthorne's friend Longfellow had recently inspired
the nation with his poem "A Psalm of Life", which
ends:

> Let us, then, be up and doing
> With a heart for any fate;
> Still achieving, still pursuing,
> Learn to labor and to wait.

And Emerson had exhorted that a man must toss "the
laws, the books, idolatries and customs out of the
window" before "we shall pity him no more, but
thank and revere him" ("Self Reliance" 1841). But
22

Hester's adherence to optimistic self-renewal contradicts her own experience and her own choice of the letter as identity even as it suggests a similar abandonment of identity to Arthur Dimmesdale [23]. It hardly needs Dimmesdale's blasphemous impulses on his way home to show us that the rhetoric of Hester's speech here is untrustworthy and a denial of the reality it attempts to persuade him of, like the false expression she wears in attracting little Pearl to her side, "arraying her face in a holiday suit of unaccustomed smiles" (I,209).

Similarly, Dimmesdale's ultimate victory over the letter, like Hester's is counterbalanced by its perpetuation: first, as Hester returns and takes it up again to wear it until she dies and second, as it glimmers above her grave, in a conclusion which stresses the written over even the emblematic: "a device, a herald's wording of which might serve for a motto and brief description of our now concluded legend; so sombre is it, and relieved only by one ever glowing point of light gloomier than the shadow:-

"ON A FIELD, SABLE, THE LETTER A, GULES"

So the book concludes, not with a successful speaking of the letter, but with yet another redaction, in which the hieroglyphic or the pictographic sign is not depicted but <u>rewritten</u> in the purely formal language of heraldry [24].

And what of the writer who hopes to erase the "deep print" of the letter out of his brain, "now that it has done its office" after being fixed there in "very undesirable distinctness" by long meditation? (I,259) The author is curiously evasive about his authorship: he hides behind the manuscript of Mr. Surveyer Pue, then admits to "dressing up" - that is embroidering - the bare facts of the narrative, only to conceal himself again by asking that the whole be considered as "The Posthumous Papers of a Decapitated Surveyer" and hoping that the sketch of the Custom-House may be readily excused in "a gentleman who writes from beyond the grave .... For I am in the realm of quiet" (I,44). Hawthorne's uneasiness about the contents of the "Custom-House" came doubtless from a suspicion that he had been too free with his revenge on the living personalities of Salem, his home town after all, but it is exactly parallel to his concern about the activity of writing,

expressed in his humourous imagination of a rebuke
from his Puritan ancestors: "No aim, that I have
ever cherished, would they recognise as laudable;
no success of mine ... would they deem otherwise
than worthless, if not positively disgraceful.
'What is he?' murmurs one gray shadow of my
forefathers to the other. 'A writer of story-books!
What kind of a business in life - what mode of
glorifying God, or being serviceable to mankind in
his day and generation - may that be?'" (I,10) The
choice of the previously mediated sign or fetish
object for the centre of his narrative is partly a
consequence of uncertainty as to the status of art,
particularly fiction, and of the writer. The
adoption of a subject for artistic elaboration
implies a shared value structure in author and
audience if the author desires to "open an
intercourse with the world". But in early
nineteenth century America the _episteme_, founded on
Scottish Common Sense philosophy, Locke, and
Hartley's doctrine of the Association of Ideas,
rendered the valorization required for art
especially problematic. Hawthorne's mysterious
object, located in actuality and freighted with
history, is both excuse and justification for
imaginative embroidery. Its "discovery" in the
second-floor room of the Custom-House is
significantly placed as a counterpoint to the theme
of the real-life novel Hawthorne will not write:
"The page of life that was spread out before me
seemed dull and commonplace, only because I had not
fathomed its deeper import. A better book than I
shall ever write was there; leaf after leaf
presenting itself to me, just as it was written out
by the reality of the flitting hour, and vanishing
as fast as it was written, only because my brain
wanted the insight and my hand the cunning to
transcribe it. At some future day, it may be, I
shall remember a few scattered fragments and broken
paragraphs, and write them down, and find the
letters turn to gold upon the page"(I,37). But the
almost irresistible claims of the actual, and the
possibility of the realism of Dickens and Trollope,
had already been preempted by the "discovery" of
the magnetic letter and by Hawthorne's claims for
the place of the imagination, which must transmute
the everyday, not merely transcribe it. Although
his account of moonlight's effects on the familiar
scene when aided by flickering fire-light is
carefully phrased so as not to challenge the
dominant taste of the period, it is nevertheless
24

implicitly putting forward the claims of the imaginative story-teller against those of the sturdy realists:

> Thus, therefore, the floor of our familiar room has become neutral territory, somewhere between the real world and fairy-land, where the Actual and the Imaginary may meet, and each imbue itself with the nature óf the other. Ghosts might enter here, without affrighting us.... [The warmer light of the coal-fire] mingles itself with the cold spirituality of the moonbeams, and communicates, as it were, a heart and sensibilities of human tenderness to the forms which fancy summons up. It converts them from snow-images into men and women. Glancing at the looking-glass, we behold - deep within its haunted verge - the smouldering glow of the half-extinguished anthracite, the white moonbeams on the floor, and a repetition of all the gleam and shadow of the picture, with one remove futher from the actual, and nearer to the imaginative. Then, at such an hour, and with this scene before him, if a man, sitting all alone, cannot dream strange things, and make them look like truth, he need never try to write romances (I,36).

Writing, as the deliberate movement "one remove further from the actual", implicates Hawthorne himself in the displacements he observes in **The Scarlet Letter**: in achieving "the imaginative" his aesthetic insists on a forfeiting of the actual, which must therefore be counterfeited by an illusion of historical presence and documentary authenticity both in the letter itself and in Pue's chronicle of Hester.

This begins to establish the complexity of Hawthorne's attitude towards the hypothesis of immediate, unmediated "presence", as against the displaced, redacted versions of experience in "twice-told" tales. The counterfeiting of the actual involved in the device of the elaborated sign testifies to his sophisticated awareness of the difficulties faced by the American genius he introduced in "A Select Party" (1844) [announced under the sign of his own impossibility, along with the other creatures of fantasy (X,66)]. In comparison with his contemporaries Hawthorne

25

Eve Tempted

appears much more "writerly", constantly intruding
the means of presentation and stressing reflection
over inspiration in his material. Whereas American
writers like Longfellow, Whittier, or Bryant strove
for a natural, unaffected, invisible style which
would so hug the contours of cultural expectation
as to be imperceptible even when engaged in complex
rhythmic schemes; and whereas the orphic
transcendentalists attempted to utter the one
self-sufficient word in which bard and thing might
merge, abjuring the "rules" of composition as so
much outworn Augustan baggage, and concealing the
metaphysical wiles of their craft beneath the
apparent innocence of tropes drawn from Nature;
Hawthorne, and to a lesser extent Melville,
developed the extravagently "written" style of
Brockden Brown and Poe. But not so much out of a
respect for forms of the past or literary tradition
did Hawthorne insist upon the protrusions of his
rhetoric, nor was he unwilling to subscribe to some
of the tenets of the transcendental reformers; his
insistence on admission of artifice was rather a
product of his scepticism and a puritan (though not
Puritanical) guilt over any lapse of integrity:
which even included the lapse inherent in the very
suggestion of its possibility.
     "Earth's Holocaust" (1844) provides an
explicit model of Hawthorne's relationship to that
possibility of integrity, finding it more in the
hangman, the "Last Thief" and the "Last Murderer"
than in the optimists who pile up the bonfire. The
combustibles chosen for the great fire amount to a
lexicon of secondariness: yesterday's news, the
badges of aristocracy and patents of nobility
(including heraldry), regal insignia, the hogsheads
of liquor that induce supplementary consciousness,
along with the stimulants of tea, coffee and
tobacco; "Everything rich and racy - all the spice
of life" says one old gentleman lamenting his now
useless pipe (X,387), and echoing the gloom of the
Last Toper, who thinks that "good-fellowship is
gone forever" in the burning of his drink (X,387).
These are followed by letters, bonds, diplomas,
sermons and codes of manners, the disparaged work
of an American author; and then the weapons of war,
along with the instruments of execution. The ardent
young leader of the incendiaries responds to
scepticism by calling, "Let the heart have its
voice here, as well as the intellect. And as for
ripeness - and as for progress, let mankind always
do the highest, kindest, noblest thing, that, at
26

any given period, it has attained to the perception
of; and surely that thing cannot be wrong, nor
wrongly timed" (X,393). Accordingly, the documents,
stocks and currency of the world are obliterated,
and the arbitrary laws encoded in written
constititutions, acts of government and statute
books are also called to be burned, although the
attempt may be unsuccessful (X,394). Much of
Hawthorne's stress falls upon the burning of
literature, adducing against the pleas of the
"desperate book worm" whose "only reality was a
bound volume" the claims that Nature is better than
any book, the human heart is deeper than any system
of philosophy, or the "great book of Time is still
spread wide open before us" and other such
apothegms worthy of a man who had known Bronson
Alcott (X,398). The addition of pamphlets from the
presses of the New World leave the earth "for the
first time since the days of Cadmus, free from the
plague of letters", but ironically, an "enviable
field for the authors of the next generation"
(X,398). Their essays in words are followed by the
Logos itself, as the Bible in its innumerable
versions is consumed by the fire; accompanied by a
mighty wind and a desolate howling, and the
transmutation of the narrator's calm companion into
a personage of dark complexion with eyes redder
than the bonfire. This ominous figure assures the
Last Murderer that the reformers have forgotten to
throw in that "foul cavern" from which all these
evils spring, the human heart (X,403). We may read
this as Hawthorne's testimony to Calvinist innate
depravity (against the grain of his professed
allegiances) or as a "deeper" psychologist's scorn
for improvements based upon merely intellectual
reform ("if we go no further than the Intellect,
and strive, with merely that feeble instrument, to
discern and rectify what is wrong, our whole
accomplishment will be a dream ..." (X,404); but it
is in either case a critique of essentialism,
through its disavowal of the possibility of
authenticity within the self, exactly comparable to
the discovery of writtenness within speech.

NOTES

1. For further discussion see, e.g. Terence
Hawkes, **Structuralism and Semiotics** (London:

Methuen & Co, 1977) pp. 19-28.

2. References in the text are to The Centenary Edition of the Works of Nathaniel Hawthorne (Columbus: Ohio State University Press, 1974), I, 31.

3. The cardinal assumption of Association Theory (introduced by Hartley in 1749 but still dominant in Hawthorne's period) was that one association would automatically call up another, according to fixed rules. I have attempted to explore some of the aesthetic implications of this doctrine in "Discovery in Poe," Delta no 12 (May, 1981) pp.1-10.

4. Hawthorne's use of hieroglyphic signs has been very well treated in John T. Irwin's American Hieroglyphics (Newhaven and London: Yale University Press, 1980) pp.239-266. On the place of writing in American Puritan culture, see Mitchell Robert Breitwieser, "Cotton Mather's Crazed Wife," Glyph 5 (1979) p.100.

5. Ursula Brumm, American Thought and Religious Typology tr. by John Hoaglund (New Brunswick: Rutgers University Press, 1971) p.126.

6. Brumm, p.24.

7. Brumm, p.126.

8. Charles Fiedelson, in Symbolism and American Literature (Chicago: University of Chicago Press, 1953) assumes a coalescence of the various meanings of the letter into one symbol, but his analysis actually establishes the difference in its meanings for different observers. See also Eric J. Sundquist, Home as Found: Authority and Genealogy in Nineteenth Century American Literature (Baltimore and London: Johns Hopkins University Press, 1979) p. 112.

9. Karl Keller, "Alephs, Zahirs, and the Triumph of Ambiguity: Typology in Nineteenth Century American Literature," in Earl Miner, ed., Literary Uses of Typology (Princeton: Princeton University Press, 1977) pp. 279,299.

10. Keller, p.300.

11. Jacques Derrida, Of Grammatology, tr. by G. C. Spivak (Baltimore and London: Johns Hopkins University Press, 1974); Jean Jacques Rousseau, Essay on the Origin of Languages, 1761. Page references in text are to the translation by J.H. Moran and A. Gode (New York: Ungar,1966).

12. Marion L. Kesselring, Hawthorne's Reading, 1828-1850 (Folcroft, Pa: The Folcroft Press, 1969 rpt of New York Public Library Bulletin 53, 1949) p. 60.

13. On natural signs see "The Psychology of Nathaniel Hawthorne," Doctoral Dissertation of John T. McKiernan, Pennsylvania State University, 1957, no 24027, pp. 83-89. Dimmesdale's stigma is, of course, a "written" extension of his gesture of clutching at his heart.

14. R.W. Emerson, "Nature," in **The Collected Works of Ralph Waldo Emerson** ed. R.E. Spiller and A.R. Ferguson (Cambridge, Mass: Belknap Press of Harvard University Press, 1971), p.28.

15. To continue this striking analogy, it will be noted that Dimmesdale (the Minister D--) conceals the letter conspicuously, where the detective knows to look for it. ("The Purloined Letter" was published in **The Gift** in 1845).

16. Irwin, p.251

17. Derrida, **Of Grammatology**, pp.173-174. See Rousseau, **Discourse on the Origin of Inequality**, 1775 (London: Dent, 1955) pp. 182-186. And compare **The Blithedale Romance**, "Nature ... a strict but loving mother...." (III,62).

18. The type of "her of Babylon," means "whore," but also, by a familiar usage of the Puritans, the Roman Catholic church, with which Hawthorne associates Hester as Madonna (I,56).

19. Derrida, p.139.

20. Derrida, p.140.

21. Millicent Bell, "The Obliquity of Signs," **Massachusetts Review** (Spring, 1982). See also John G. Bayer's article, "Narrative Techniques and the Oral Tradition in **The Scarlet Letter**," **American Literature** 52, no 2 (May, 1980).

22. "The Celestial Railroad" (X,186)

23. The exactness of the parallel is increased by the fact that the original scarlet letters were "AD": Dimmesdale's initials. The text of the law of Plymouth, 1636, holds that "Whosoever shall comitt Adultery shalbee severely punished by whiping two sevrall times ... and likewise to weare two Capitall letters viz. AD cut out in cloth and sewed on theire upermost Garments on their arme or back...." **The American Notebooks of Nathaniel Hawthorne** ed. by Randall Stewart (New Haven: Yale University Press, 1932) p.229. So Dimmesdale's abandonment of his name, AD, would be the same as Hester's abandonment of the Letter.

24. Heraldry has a subtle importance throughout **The Scarlet Letter**: there is an early reference to the arms of Hester's English family and another to the crest of Pearl's husband ("bearings unknown to English heraldry," I,26); as well as the sign on

the tombstone. Hester's stark "A" is appropriate to the new world as a coat of arms: a schematic, abecedarian device which posits abstractions as the essentials of the American identity and locates that identity in guilt and defiance. So the liberation from aristocratic hierarchy enjoyed in the new land is paid for in the invention of new forms of repression. D. Greenwood also discusses "The Heraldic device in The Scarlet Letter," in American Literature 46 (1974-5) pp. 207-10.

Can Hawthorne's scepticism be seen in a wider perspective? The great philosophical debate of the age can be described as a debate between Sensationalism and Intuitionalism, in the double antagonisms first evidenced in the supersession of Lockean sensationalist thought by Scottish Common Sense appeals to innate propensities (i.e. the moral sense), and second, the limited acceptance of Kantian (Transcendentalist) ideas of innate categories, as among the American coteries known intimately to Hawthorne. In each dispute the importance of essentialist thought can be seen: the Common Sense critics of Lockean Sensationalist thought (Brown, Stewart, Reid) held that later sophistications of Lockean theory or Hartley's doctrine of the Association of ideas by "infidels" such as Hume, and proponents of materialism such as Lavatar or Combe, Spurzheim and Gall or Condillac, had demonstrated a crucial weakness in the model of knowledge through sensation and reflection which would only be redressed by an appeal to a universal experience of an <u>inherent</u> moral sense in mankind. Hawthorne belonged largely to this school of thought, through his education at Bowdoin College and his later reading in Dugald Steward, Thomas Brown and David Hartley [1]. Adherents of Kantian theory, or rather of its more colourful modulations through Fichte and Schilling via Cousin and Coleridge, proposed a more sweeping commitment to immediate, direct knowledge of the immaterial and the eternal. A quotation from Laurens Perseus Hickock, one of the less restrained philosophical voluptuaries, will illustrate: "In this science [rational psychology] we pass from the facts of experience wholly out beyond it, and seek for the <u>rationale</u> of experience itself in the necessary and

31

universal principles which must be conditional for
all facts of a possible experience.... In the
conclusion of this science it becomes competent for
us to affirm, not as from mere experience we may,
that this is, but, from these necessary and
universal principles, that this must be" [2]. The
familiar credo of the Transcendentalists had its
roots in such assertions of inevitable principles
of being but flowered more spectacularly in the
orphic sayings of Emerson's circle: "It is the
perpetual effort of conscience to divorce the soul
from the dominion of sense; to nullify the
dualities of the apparent, and restore the
intuition of the real.... Understanding notes
diversity; conscience alone divines unity, and
integrates all experience in identity of spirit."
Thus Bronson Alcott in The Dial, (July, 1840)[3].
     After his period at the Old Manse, Concord;
his friendship with William Ellery Channing; and
through his wife's sister, Elizabeth Peabody, as
well as his own experience at Transcendental Farm,
Hawthorne was thoroughly exposed to romantic
philosophy. His position is generally that of the
child who perceives the true cut of the Emperor's
clothes, feeling that the seen has more credibility
than the unseen, as in his bemused description of
the prophet's adherents in "The Old Manse" (1846):

> These hobgoblins of flesh and blood were
> attracted thither by the wide-spreading
> influence of a great original Thinker, who had
> his earthly abode at the opposite extremity of
> our village. His mind acted upon other minds,
> of a certain constitution, with wonderful
> magnetism, and drew many men upon long
> pilgrimages, to speak with him face to face.
> Young visionaries - to whom just so much of
> insight had been imparted, as to make life all
> labyrinth around them - came to seek the clue
> that should guide them out of their
> self-involved bewilderment. Gray-headed
> theorists - whose system, at first air, had
> finally imprisoned them in an iron framework -
> travelled painfully to his door, not to ask
> deliverance, but to invite this free spirit
> into their own thraldom. People that had
> lighted on a new thought, or a thought that
> they fancied new, came to Emerson, as the
> finder of a glittering gem hastens to a
> lapidary, to ascertain its quality and value.
> Uncertain, troubled, earnest wanderers,

through the midnight of the moral world, beheld his intellectual fire, as a beacon burning on a hill-top, and climbing the difficult ascent, looked forth into the surrounding obscurity, more hopefully than hitherto. The light revealed objects unseen before - mountains, gleaming lakes, glimpses of a creation among the chaos - but also, as was unavoidable, it attracted bats and owls, and the host of night-birds, which flapped their dusky wings against the gazers eyes, and sometimes were mistaken for fowls of angelic feather. Such delusions always hover nigh, whenever a beacon-fire of truth is kindled (X 30,31).

Hawthorne's satire turns back upon Emersonian philosophy the very displacements it claimed to evade: it attracts theorists, whose own systems inexorably bind them; visionaries whose bewilderment is self-involved and turns their lives to labyrinths; obsessive collectors of ideas and connoisseurs of the intellect who perceive thought as material, fit for valuation in terms of its rarity or refinement. Hawthorne compares the new doctrine to a beacon-fire (traditional warning of invasion as well as celebration) which attracts the darker aspects of romantic thought as much as the angelic inspirations for which they are mistaken. Thus the assiduous cultivation of inner truth leads to ossification in systematic dogma; all the new development of high thought is crystallised or calcified, and the sleep of reason produces monsters as well as sublime vistas and the sense of creation among the chaos. He ironically concludes that there had been times of his life when he might have asked Emerson for the "master-word, that should solve me the riddle of the universe," but now, "being happy, I felt as if there were no question to be put, and therefore admired Emerson as a poet of deep beauty and austere tenderness, but sought nothing from him as a philosopher" (X,31).

On the other hand, if we take his description of the old works of divinity stored in the attic of the Manse as a guide, Hawthorne cared just as little for the authority of the established American tradition, whether Puritan or Unitarian in persuasion. His comments on the dreary mass of old volumes and new pamphlets amount to a critique of the written on the grounds of its unreadability;

its "illegible short-hand" might perhaps conceal matter of proud truth and wisdom but to judge by the material that could be made out, any such expectation was doomed to be thwarted: "...I burrowed among these venerable books, in search of any living thought, which should burn like a coal of fire, or glow like an inextinguishable gem, beneath the dead trumpery that had long hidden it. But I found no such treasure; all was dead alike .... Thought grows mouldy" (X,19). Hawthorne is struck by the materiality of this reading fodder, just as Melville was later struck by the writtenness of his folios of whales: the vast folio body of Divinity is "too corpulent ... to comprehend the spiritual element of religion," and has the appearance of books of enchantment (X,18) [4]. The pocket volumes filled with Greek and Latin quotations impressed him "as if they had been intended for very large ones, but had been unfortunately blighted, at an early stage of their growth" (X,19). The secret preoccupation of these texts with their own status as objects, expressed in substantiality and heavy investments in black leather, provides the basis for a criticism of their failures of inner light. In comparison, only the most ephemeral of writing, the old newspapers and almanacs, retained any "sap", provoking Hawthorne to speculate that "a work of genius is but the newspaper of a century, or perchance of a hundred centuries" (X,21). This much essentiality, of living for the moment, is allowed by him, and next to it we may place his estimation of the possibility of grace: "so long as an unlettered soul can attain to saving grace, there would seem to be no deadly error in holding theological libraries to be accumulations of, for the most part, stupendous impertinence" (X,19) [5].

Dimly looming behind these remarks appears the old Puritan controversy between faith and works, and Hawthorne's vestigial adherence to the doctrine of salvation through grace rather than self-improvement and good deeds. This underlies his sympathy with the Last Thief and the Last Murderer of "Earth's Holocaust," who suggest the companions of Christ's crucifixion, and his scepticism as to any possibility of essential integrity except one which recognises the displacements at the very core of the self. Books, dogmas, and objects are proposed as hazardous supplements to the problematic truth, soul or "heart" which is itself scrutinised in the fiction. Once we see the severity with which Hawthorne investigates interiority we can no longer accept the irreducibility of the concept of the "heart" but must review the whole issue of essence versus exteriority and thereby come to some rather startling conclusions as to his "meanings" [6].

A primary locus for the consideration of this issue is "The Artist of the Beautiful" (1844), collected in **Mosses From an Old Manse** (1846), the volume of stories which extensively demonstrates Hawthorne's lasting preoccupation with the problematics of inner and outer, substance and essence. The artist, Owen Warland, struggles to articulate his opposition to the materialistic society within which he lives, a society ruled by "that order of sagacious understandings who think that life should be regulated, like clockwork, with leaden weights" and which is presented through the metaphor of the clock, which controls merchants, nurses, and lovers alike (X,454). Peter Hovenden, his erstwhile master as a watchmaker, and Robert Danforth, the blacksmith who wins Owen's idealised Annie, alike oppress this artist of mechanical miniatures, by their cynicism and brute forcefulness, respectively. Annie Hovenden, not fine enough in her responses to satisfy Owen's ideal, still retains his devotion and receives the fabulous mechanical butterfly as her belated wedding gift. It is, however, crushed by her child, who bears a look of his grandfather Peter Hovenden's chilling sagacity along with the innocence of childhood.

The simple framework of this story seems to oppose delicacy, dedication and the pursuit of spirituality and beauty, to materialism, grossness, cynicism, and physical strength. Whenever Owen despairs of success in achieving the great aim of spiritualisation of mechanism he undergoes a transformation into a lower form of organization, becoming dull and commonplace, or corpulent and childish "as if the spirit had gone out of him, leaving the body to flourish in a sort of vegetable existence" (X, 465); or, on another disappointment, becoming an inebriate in order to overcome "a certain irksomeness of spirit which ... was more intolerable than any fantastic miseries and horror that the abuse of wine could summon up" (X, 461). The moralized narration presents Owen Warland's ultimate achievement of the precious mechanical butterfly as a transcendence of the limits of the earthly, leaving him secure against the brutalities

of the world as these are expressed through the
child's violence:

> The blacksmith, by main force, unclosed the
> infant's hand, and found within the palm a
> small heap of glittering fragments, whence the
> Mystery of Beauty had fled for ever. And as
> for Owen Warland, he looked placidly at what
> seemed the ruin of his life's labour, and
> which was yet no ruin. He had caught a far
> other butterfly than this. When the artist
> rose high enough to achieve the Beautiful, the
> symbol by which he made it perceptible to
> mortal senses became of little value in his
> eyes, while his spirit possessed itself in the
> enjoyment of the Reality (X,475).

That is, the artist, having achieved the essence of
the beautiful, is enabled to dispense with the
materiality within which it was embodied.
    But here again is the idea of substitution:
the butterfly is a signifier, the signified is
transcendent Beauty; Owen can be liberated from the
spell of the sign by apprehension of its referent.
But is there not another substitution involved in
this series; the substitution of the butterfly for
Annie? It must be apparent that the butterfly
substitutes for Annie not only in the final scene,
in which Owen is shown triumphant, but always and
necessarily, for he "had persisted in connecting
all his dreams of artistical success with Annie's
image; she was the visible shape in which the
spiritual power that he worshipped, and on whose
altar he hoped to lay a not unworthy offering, was
made manifest to him" (X,464). What Annie is, or
may be, is shown as secondary to what she
represents, a "spiritual power" to be approached
through the "artistical" medium. The narrative is
not deficient in commentary upon this aspect of his
quest: as is usual in Hawthorne, the problem rather
lies in a surplus of explicit commentary. "Of
course" he had deceived himself; there were no such
attributes in Annie Hovenden as his imagination had
endowed her with" (X,464). Or, on the other hand:
"Poor Owen Warland! He had indeed erred, yet
pardonably; for if any human spirit could have
sufficiently reverenced the processes so sacred in
his eyes, it must have been a woman's. Even Annie
Hovenden, possibly, might not have disappointed
him, had she been enlightened by the deep
intelligence of love" (X,460). Owen's insistence on
36

the supplement, however, is an act of violence against that hypothetical "love", for when Annie gives a minute mechanism the slightest possible touch with her needle [7],"the artist seized her by the wrist with a force that made her scream aloud. She was affrighted at the convulsion of intense rage and anguish that writhed across his features" (X,460). The butterfly was "for Annie," but Annie is sacrificed to the butterfly, and it in turn is sacrificed to the idea which it represents. Just as the artificial butterfly is preferred to the real butterfly of nature, so is Warland's "artistical" quest preferred to the love it pretends to serve. In oblique commentary on this sits the baby, a combination of natural innocence and sagacity inherited, not from Owen's successful rival Danforth, but through Annie from her father Peter Hovenden, who values his silver watch almost as much as he does his daughter (X, 456). One begins to suspect that Owen Warland's struggle is to reproduce nature without its impurities; the butterfly without its insect anatomy, life without its mortality and physical embodiment. So the preference for the supplement is also a preference for death and Owen, the very prototype of the Romantic artist, is himself subject to a fundamental romantic critique. The narrative rather ostentatiously reminds the reader of Albertus Magnus's Man of Brass, and the Brazen Head of Friar Bacon; also the coach and horses manufactured for the Dauphin of France and a clockwork fly and mechanical duck; it does not, however, mention the story of Pygmalion or Hoffman's Olympia: perhaps because these two tales of automatons illuminate too brightly the narcissism that is being suppressed within the tale [8]. Rather than an approved figure of the triumphant artist, Owen Warland develops into yet another practitioner of the flight into secondariness.

In "The Artist of the Beautiful" life flows into the rigidity of a mechanical signifier, just as in The Scarlet Letter life - even we might say, blood - flows into the emblem of the letter [9]. Here it is rigidified or congealed, and the persons who might organise and use the sign are themselves used by it. Similar systems of entrapment operate in "Rappaccini's Daughter," a tale of the same year, (1844). In "Rappaccini's Daughter" the pattern of displacement begins as early as the title; Beatrice is not named as herself but as the single member of a category announced under the father's name. As the narrative develops the "essence" of Beatice is located at further and further removes: as an inhabitant of the garden; a beautiful girl; a gorgeous shrub; a broken fountain; the Beatrice of Dante; a departed spirit. Although these extrojections are implicit in her situation as a woman who has been rendered physically poisonous or a new Eve in a fallen world, the agent of their elucidation is Giovanni, who is himself a creator and victim of the system of exclusions, denials and displacements. Giovanni is presented through a double narrative movement: in the first part he is proposed as the consciousness through which the reader must apprehend Beatrice and the garden, subject to the confusions and limitations of sensory evidence and human prejudice; whereas in the second part the narrator asserts unequivocally that Beatrice is an angel (X,122), or that his (and the reader's) earthly doubts amount, like Rappaccini's poisonous intrusion, to a defilement of the "pure whiteness of Beatrice's image" (X,120)[10]. Giovanni is criticised for his failure to sustain the height of spirit to which his "earthly" enthusiasm of passion had exalted him (X,120); his breath is "imbued with a venomous feeling out of his heart" (X,122), and Beatrice asks "Oh, was there not, from the first, more poison in thy nature than in mine?" (X,127).

The terms in which such discriminations are offered constitute a whole vocabulary of inner and outer; surface and depth; material and spiritual; artificial and natural; love and lust; beauty and ugliness dualities, and reintroduce the notion of a hierarchy of truth in which the visual lies at one extreme, transcended by the spoken, which is in turn subordinate to the gestural, here exemplified in touch. Beatrice bids Giovanni "Believe nothing of me save what you see with your own eyes" but accepts his correction: "Bid me believe nothing save what comes from your own lips." "I do so bid you, signor," she replied. "Forget whatever you have fancied in regard to me. If true to the outward senses, still it may be false in its essence; but the words of Beatrice Rappaccini's lips are true from the depths of the heart outward. Those you may believe" (X,111,112). The primary position of touch in this series is attested by the trace of Beatrice' hand on Giovanni's arm, still imprinted the morning after she has grasped him, and by the insistence with which she eludes his embraces, never even allowing her dress to
38

touch him. Giovanni congratulates himself that he
is "no flower to perish in her grasp" at the very
moment of realization that the flowers he has held
are dying (X,121). But all of these terms are then
superseded by the concept of inward vision: "A
fervor glowed in her whole aspect, and beamed upon
Giovanni's consciousness like the light of truth
itself ... he seemed to gaze through the beautiful
girl's eyes into her transparent soul, and felt no
more doubt or fear" (X,112). The most heavily
stressed valuation of Beatrice combines the
integrity of the spoken with the idealised vision
of the inner eye, in a metaphor drawn from the
fountain: "recollections of many a holy and
passionate outgush of her heart, when the pure
fountain had been unsealed from its depths, and
made visible in its transparency to his mental eye;
recollections which, had Giovanni known how to
estimate them, would have assured him that all this
ugly mystery was but an earthly illusion, and that,
whatever mist of evil might seem to have gathered
over her, the real Beatrice was a heavenly angel"
(X,122). But Giovanni does not so estimate her,
trapped within the inflections of the secondary he
cannot evade his own reflection, "white and
marble," and "the likeness of something frightful"
(X,121). The narcissistic passion which constitutes
his feeling for Beatrice, "that cunning semblance
of love which flourishes in the imagination, but
strikes no depth of root into the heart" (X,115),
provokes again a series of substitutions: like
Dimmesdale and Warland he prefers death to giving
himself to the other.
   There is a significant opposition between the
sealed silver vial given by Baglioni, and the pure
spiritual fountain represented by Beatrice: The
one is a stale relic of the past (made by Benvenuto
Cellini, famous not only for his skills as a
craftsman but also for his adulterous adventures
and his dabbling in black magic, as reported in his
Autobiography [11],) containing the distilled
alembic of science; the other is an ever refreshed
source of beauty and virtue, indifferent to
whatever material habitation it may be given, like
the fountain in the garden (X,94). The complexity
of this antagonism is deepened by Giovanni's
reference to holy water as they stand beside the
fountain in thir final encounter: "Yes, yes; let us
pray! Let us to church, and dip our figures in the
holy water at the portal! They that come after us
will perish as by a pestilence. Let us sign crosses

in the air! It will be scattering curses abroad in the likeness of holy symbols" (X,124). So the matter of inner and outer becomes a question of essence and containment, and finally a matter of sign and meaning: can the sign of the cross be a secret curse; can the outwardly fair be demonic, or the outwardly polluted be angelic; and can the terms of these questions be sufficiently stabilised even to allow their asking? The problem is akin to that in **Hamlet**: how to propose the meaning of the "natural" once the "natural" has been completely destabilised by "something rotten in the state of Denmark" [12]. In **Hamlet** the difficulty eventuates in a perturbation of form (the play is long and deficient in dramatic action in terms of the revenge-formula), and similarly here the problem is solved forcibly by the definitive statements of the narrator, violently insisting on the priority of innerness, and transcending the category of the "natural" – which has been suborned by Rappaccini's adulterous mixings of species (X,110), as well as by Giovanni's lust – by the category of the "spiritual", the narrowing of Beatrice's identity by a denial of her earthly qualities in favour of her heavenly soul; resulting in her eventual flight from the world. Her death is the emptying of a signifier which never gave an unambiguous meaning except that forced upon it by the narrator: Giovanni's "beautiful, shall I call her? – or inexpressibly terrible?" (X,103), being closer to the sustained oppositions of the text than the narrator's desperate overcontrol.

The most internally consistent version of the Edenic allegory suggested in the story casts Beatrice as Adam, Giovanni as Eve, and Rappaccini and Baglioni as God and the Devil respectively, with Baglioni's vial as the apple of knowledge. This allegory supposes that absolute goodness in a postlapsarian world would appear as absolute evil; hence the innocent garden would be poisonous to mortals and other tainted creatures of the fallen world [13]. Such a version has the merit of systematic inversion: good stands for evil and male for female. But as soon as the narrator (and Beatrice) disown materiality and poisonous external appearances, the nature of "good" in the inverted model becomes discredited. Is this perhaps then a gnostic allegory, in which the serpent is to be applauded for encouraging mankind to find knowledge, thus freeing him from oppression? [14]:

The first Archon, (Ialdabaoth) brought Adam (created by the Archons) and placed him in paradise which paradise which he said to be a "delight" for him: that is, he intended to deceive him. For their delight is bitter and their beauty is lawless. Their fruit is poison against which there is no cure, and their promise is death to him. Yet their tree was planted as "tree of life": I shall disclose to you the mystery of their "life" - it is their Counterfeit Spirit, which originated from them so as to turn him away, so that he might not know his perfection. [15]

Baglioni, however, seems an unworthy agent for gnosis, as his jealous and even malevolent designs against Rappaccini are underscored: "...it is too insufferable an impertinence in Rappaccini, thus to snatch the lad out of my own hands, as I may say, and make use of him for his infernal experiments. This daughter of his! It shall be looked to!" (X,108). Baglioni is more like a version of (Milton's) Satan than the vehicle of "the transcendent principle" in its first success against the evil "principle of the world, which is vitally interested in preventing knowledge in man as the inner worldly hostage of Light." In the gnostic interpretation the action of the serpent "marks the beginning of all gnosis on earth which thus by its very origin is stamped as opposed to the world and its God, and indeed, as a form of rebellion." [16]. Perhaps Hawthorne was deeply drawn to such secret readings of the creation myth as he might find in the ancient theological volumes of the Old Manse. We can see his allegory here as a critique of both the orthodox and heretical versions, stressing man's unworthiness and limited capacity for good. The temptation in the garden cannot finally be viewed as a positive stage; true, the garden is full of poisonous fruit, represented especially by the gorgeous shrub with its gemlike blossoms, but the awakening comes not from eating this fruit but from accepting an "antidote" from outside Eden. Hawthorne refuses the case for "God" and for "Satan" in reviewing the myth, and presents Beatrice's fall as an ascent into paradise beyond her father's or any earthly version: "I am going, father, where the evil, which thou hast striven to mingle with my being, will pass away like a dream - like the fragrance of these poisonous flowers, which will no longer taint my breath among the flowers of Eden" (X,127). The reworked myth is intractable: it requires a further "real" paradise which carries the authority of the narration, that is, the certainty of Beatrice's angelism insisted upon by the narrator, against Giovanni's persistent, ultimately fatal, doubts.

Perhaps the ponderous humour of the introduction should after all be taken seriously: its author masquerades frivolously as M. de l'Aubepine, a little known writer best described by his negative features. He is too remote, shadowy and unsubstantial to suit popular tastes; but too popular to satisfy transcendentalists. His love of allegory steals the warmth from his conceptions and leaves them like "scenery and people in the clouds"; his stories are sometimes historical, sometimes contemporary, and sometimes "so far as can be discovered, have little or no reference to either time or space." Occasionally, "a breath of nature, a raindrop of pathos and tenderness, or a gleam of humour, will find its way into the midst of his fantastic imagery...." Such a concern to disappear, or translate himself and his works, provides a framework within which the narrator's insistently categorical assurances are questioned, if not denied. But that questioning is, of course, undertaken by the author himself. Rappaccini's poisonous garden anticipates the actually poisonous gardens which Hawthorne discovered in his later visit to Italy. The same issues occupied him then, but the answers turned out to be even less categorical than those in his early tales. And before then, **The House of the Seven Gables** opened up uncertainties that he was unable to resolve, in its enquiries into the possibility of naturalness or innocence.

NOTES

1. Allan Gardner Smith, **The Analysis of Motives** (Amsterdam: Rodopi, 1980) pp. 76-119. Marion Kesselring, **Hawthorne's Reading** (Folcroft, Pa: The Folcroft Press, 1969 rpt of New York Public Library Bulletin 53, 1949) pp.45,53,62.
2.Samuel Schmucker, **Rational Psychology** 1848 (Rev ed. New York: Ivison, 1870) p. 14.
3. In Perry Miller, ed., **The American**

Transcendentalists: Their Prose and Poetry (New York: Doubleday Anchor, 1957) pp. 89,90.

4. Hawthorne associated enchantment with materialism, as is clear in **The House of the Seven Gables** and **The Blithedale Romance**, as well as his letter to Sophia on the subject of mesmeric healing for migraine. In **Love Letters of Nathaniel Hawthorne** (Chicago: The Society of the Dofobs, 1907) II, p. 62.

5. Although the underlying tenets of the Common Sense philosophers were so familiar to Hawthorne as to be almost invisible to him, the stupefying religiosity and complacence of their assumptions about human nature did not escape him. Most American psychologists at this time were also ministers, concerned to pursue truth right up to its conflict with religion before abandoning the struggle. See Smith, **The Analysis of Motives**, p. 155. So Hawthorne's criticism of the theological library is also a criticism of the status quo in psychology.

6. Refusing, for example, to rest with such notions as that: "...we find in **The Scarlet Letter** a thoroughgoing commitment to reverence for the human heart, which in the course of the novel develops into a commitment to reverence for the whole truth about the heart." John F. Becker, **Hawthorne's Historical Allegory** (New York: Kennikat Press, 1971) p. 165.

7. Hawthorne uses needles, and sewing, as symbols of femininity (see, for example, IV,39,40). Perhaps there is a suggestion of phallic symbolism here, as in Owen's detached signifier.

8. Freud analyses the story of Olympia in "Das Unheimliche" (**Imago**, 5, 1919), **The Complete Psychological Works of Sigmund Freud** , translated by James Strachey (London: The Hogarth Press, 1955), vol XVII, pp. 217-253. Paul de Man discusses Pygmalion and Galathea in ways relevant to this study in **Allegories of Reading** (New Haven: Yale University Press, 1979).

9. **The Scarlet Letter** was written at a time of traumatic stress for Hawthorne: it was part of his response to the death of his mother (see Robert Cantwell, **Nathaniel Hawthorne, The American Years** (New York: Rinehart & Co, 1948) pp.429-431. Rudolph Von Abele notices, in **The Death of the Artist** (The Hague:Nijhoff, 1955) p.55, that there may be a reference to menstruation implied in the bloodstained rag. Another intriguing area of speculation is the relation of the story to the

secrecy of Hawthorne's engagement, the reasons for which do not seem to have been clear even to Sophia.

10. See M. L. Ross, "What Happens in Rappaccini's Garden" American Literature 43, pp.336-345.

11. Cellini's Memoirs (London: Bell, 1889). Hawthorne notes having read this in the American Notebooks Centenary Edition vol XIV (Columbus, Ohio: Ohio State University Press, 1980), p. 321.

12. " 'tis an unweeded garden / That grows to seed; things rank and gross in nature / Possess it merely." Hamlet I, ii, 134-7. The question of Gertrude's sexuality is at the bottom of Hamlet's indecision, as Beatrice's sexuality is at the root of "Rappaccini's Daughter." The flower symbolism of Ophelia is transferred to Beatrice, as is the model of death when spurned. The stress on poisons, unnatural fathers, and the exotic setting in Padua, as well as the figure of the nurse and pander Elizabeth, similarly echoe Shakespeare rather than Dante.

13. To see Adam as female is no odder than to accept the inversion of good and evil proposed in postlapsarian metaphysics.

14. Hans Jonas, "Eve and the Serpent in Gnostic Allegory," The Gnostic Religion (Boston: Beacon Press, 1958) pp. 92-94.

15. From the Apocrypha of John: 55. 18-56.See Jonas, p.93.

3   IMMURED IN THE PAST:
     THE HOUSE OF THE SEVEN GABLES

Like the Rome of **The Marble Faun** the House of
the Seven Gables occupies a previously Edenic
space, but one which is inscribed by history and
posits the problem of renewal, or redoing the past.
The house is built upon a garden plot that is
already soiled by the abuse of Matthew Maule's
rights as first owner and builder of a cottage on
the site, and his persecution as a supposed wizard
by the first American Pyncheon. When Matthew Maule
built his house he chose an Arcadian spot: "a
natural spring of soft and pleasant water – a rare
treasure on the sea-girt peninsula, where the
puritan settlement was made – had early induced
[him] to build a hut, shaggy with thatch..." (II,6)
[1]. The site is thus marked as having an original
innocence, which is not violated by the shaggy hut
with its connotations of naturalness. This space
then becomes defiled by history, so that the pure
waters of the spring turn brackish and productive
of illness, and the house subsequently erected by
Colonel Pyncheon is popularly supposed to be
haunted by the ghost of old Maule, which has a sort
of right to the apartments because they include his
old home within them. "The terror and ugliness of
Maule's crime, and the wretchedness of his
punishment, would darken the freshly plastered
walls, and infect them with the scent of an old and
melancholy house. Why, then – while so much of the
soil around him was bestrewn with the virgin forest
leaves – why should Colonel Pyncheon prefer a site
that had already been accurst?" (II,9) This was
also the question that so much interested Hawthorne
in **The Marble Faun**: how could any sort of renewal
be possible in history, in a place defiled by
generations of experience and by repetitions of the

old crimes of humanity? In the guardedly optimistic
House of the Seven Gables, as in the later Italian
romance, the answer is sought in reenactment, but
reenactment with an essential difference that will
somehow undo the knot of the past and free its
inheritors for a different future.

In **The Scarlet letter** the forest scene is a
reenactment of Hester and Dimmesdale's original
passion, with the conclusive difference of Pearl's
presence in their relationship. That one difference
is everything, however, for it plunges the lovers
into history by imposing its consequences on their
action. In **The Marble Faun** Donatello and Miriam
reenact the originary overthrowing of the
incestuous father, repeating the Cenci story, in
Shelley's version of which (1819) it is planned to
kill the father by throwing him into a chasm.
Again, the difference is significant: by his action
Donatello frees Miriam from her past, and wins his
own humanity. In **The House of the Seven Gables**
Maule's descendant Holgrave and Phoebe Pyncheon
repeat the experience of Matthew Maule and Alice
Pyncheon, when Holgrave mesmerises Phoebe, as
Mathhew had mesmerised Alice. Holgrave however
chooses not to exploit his possession of the girl,
and brings her out of the incipient trance state.
This constitutes an undoing of the knot of the
past, permitting a new union between the two
families. If this strategy seems more hollow in **The
House of the Seven Gables** than in the other
romances it may be because, on the one hand the
problem is propounded more historically as the
problem of large scale economic inequality and
inheritance, and is therefore less believably
redressed by symbolic resolution; and, on the
other, its resolution is so forced as to seem a
mere mechanical plot device. These difficulties
obscure the suggestiveness of the reenactment motif
as an encountering and redressing of neurotic
experience, resembling the therapy of recollection
and recognition later established by psychoanalysis
[2]; they also frustrate the satisfactions of
formal recuperation offered by less insistent
repetitions like the scaffold scenes in **The Scarlet
Letter.**

The theme of inequality in wealth and
inheritance stretched Hawthorne's artistic
resources in a way that even political history did
not, and found him incapable of fully responding.
There is some textual evidence that he became aware
of this himself between beginning the book and
46

defending it afterwards in the preface: in his
early pages he introduces himself as "a writer, who
endeavours to represent nature, its various
attitudes and circumstances, in a reasonably
correct outline and true coloring" (II,41), which
suggests a Dickensian ambition, whereas in the
preface he is concerned to claim the privileges of
romance rather than the obligations of the novel
which he thought "presumed to aim at a very minute
fidelity, not merely to the possible, but to the
probable and ordinary course of man's experience"
(II,1). Hawthorne had, in this work, run head on
into the contradiction between the conclusions
required by his personal integrity and political
convictions, and those required by his public (as
he conceived it) and his own desire to write a less
gloomy work than **The Scarlet Letter**. But the
materials he had chosen were simply intractable to
the kind of symnbolic resolution that he had found
effective in dealing with individual psychology or
political turning points in which the "personality"
of the nation took shape. Economic history was not
so susceptible to this kind of symbolic
reorientation, so it is not simply, as some readers
have thought, a matter of the ending; the
difficulty is structural, an incompatability
between the unredressable economic and historical
wrong, and the chosen method of retrieval.

Others besides Hawthorne fell into the same
slough, producing some of the least attractive
ideologies of the American renaissance: Emerson,
for example, attempted to reconcile economic
inequality with his system of natural beneficence
by imposing a symbolic reading of wealth which
amounted to an aggressive naturalization of the
status quo. Property is like snow, he said, "if it
fall level today it will be blown into drifts
tomorrow." In another aphorism he concluded that
economic suffering was a necessary scourge, needed
most by those who suffered from it most : "Debt,
grinding debt, whose iron face the widow, the
orphan, and the sons of genius fear and hate ... is
a preceptor whose lessons cannot be forgone, and is
needed most by those who suffer from it most" [3].

Thoreau also attempted to negotiate the
inequalities of his society, by a double stratagem:
on one side he denied the usefulness of wealth,
which could be recast as a burden; on the other
side he argued that the necessities of life were
freely available to all in his society, given a
modicum of self reliance. This attempt to turn

attention away from the razor sharp inequalities of the society did not prevent him from seeing that exploitation and economic cruelty were prevalent, as in his remark that the sleepers of the railroad were those that its construction had killed [4]. Similarly most of the economic reformers of Hawthorne's acquaintance at Brook Farm thought that economic behaviour might be changed by the example of an advanced Christian model. Hawthorne of course knew better, having noted in **The Blithedale Romance** that the reformers stood "in a position of new hostility, rather than new brotherhood," as regarded the larger society (III,20). As the advanced model of society had taken his savings, requiring Hawthorne to sue Ripley and Dana in March 1846 to get even a partial repayment [5], Hawthorne had every reason to feel the inadequacy of such arguments. Perhaps only Brownson of all the transcendental reformers was able to confront the issue with an idea of the difficulty of its placid amelioration: "And now begins the struggle between the operative and his employer, between wealth and labor" [6]. Hawthorne would not go so far as this, deploring violent remedies for injustice as worse than the evil itself. Yet **The House of the Seven Gables** indicates, in its many unassimilated contradictions, that radical perceptions were in his mind, if not such radical remedies. He states, for example, that "In this Republican country, amid the fluctuating waves of our social life, somebody is always at the drowning point" (II,38). The Preface suggests as a moral for the story "the folly of tumbling down an avalanche of ill-gotten gold, or real estate, on the heads of an unfortunate posterity, thereby to maim and crush them, until the accumulated mass shall be scattered abroad in its original atoms" (II,2). The narrator also asks the "awful query, whether each inheritor of the property - conscious of wrong, and failing to rectify it - did not commit anew the great guilt of his ancestor, and incur all its original responsibilities?" (II,20): a kind of economic original sin. Yet this is not, of course, the import of the novel's plot resolution, whereby Clifford and Hepzibah accept the Judge's avalanche of ill-gotten gold, sharing it with Phoebe, and therefore Holgrave, who turns conservative in his opinions. True, the inheritance is, in part, a restitution of the rightful property of the Maules to a Maule descendant, and a repayment of an inheritance that should have been Clifford's

Immured in the Past

before. But it is evasive to pretend that Judge
Pyncheon's "weight of sin" does not include
innumerable other economic wrongdoings. If Judge
Pyncheon is indeed like his ancestor, "bold,
imperious, crafty, laying his purposes deep ...
trampling on the weak, and ... doing his utmost to
beat down the strong" he stands as a type of
financial chicanery, and his legacy cannot be
cleaned by handing it over en masse to one of his
victims. More, the wrong is structural, as
Hawthorne has taken pains to show: "There is
something so massive, stable, and almost
irresistibly imposing, in the exterior presentment
of established rank and great possessions, that
their very existence seems to give them a right to
exist; at least, so excellent a counterfeit of
right, that few poor and humble men have force
enough to question it, even in their secret minds"
(II,25). Not only the Pycheons, then, but obviously
the rich more generally have a questionable right
to their rank and possessions. Still, the
establishing of a conception of "right" to wealth
and rank does enable a strategic retreat from the
incendiary nature of such opinions: there is a
rightful inheritance, not only a corrupt
accumulation. This seems in part to legitimate the
restitution that concludes the book, although it
cannot completely close up the avenue of
speculative inquiry opened up by the recognition
that the Pyncheon claims are fraudulent.
     Phoebe's insight into the hypocrisy of the
Judge's character plunges her into perplexity. She
wonders whether "judges, clergymen, and other
characters of that eminent stamp and
respectability, could really, in any single
instance, be otherwise than just and upright men"
(II,131). Her naive reaction enables the narrator
to adopt a much more cynical and worldy wise
position, commenting that "Dispositions more boldly
speculative may derive a stern enjoyment from the
discovery, since there must be evil in the world,
that a high man is as likely to grasp his share of
it as a low one. A wider scope of view, and a
deeper insight, may see rank, dignity, and station,
all proved illusory, so far as regards their claim
to human reverence, and yet not feel as if the
universe were thereby tumbled headlong into chaos"
(II,131). This perception of secret moral defection
is characteristic of Hawthorne, and offers safer
ground than the economic critique because it allows
for the possibility of individual moral
49

improvement; whereas the kernel of the economic argument must be that inherited and dishonestly obtained concentrations of wealth are the bane of society, the curse of Arcadia, and their redressal would require a new order which could not be presented in a light and humorous novel except, as in The Blithedale Romance, in the form of satire.

Hawthorne's writing proceeds by saturation, of which repetition and reenactment are condensed, or coalesced, forms. The House of the Seven Gables is saturated with the idea of inheritance, which endlessly proliferates and develops further implications. The inheritance of property and wealth provides the occasion for the story, but this is only the stimulus to a prolonged meditation on the inheritance of other qualities, both tangible and intangible. In this concept Hawthorne had found a key to his artistic conundrum: how to "connect a by-gone time with the very Present that is flitting away from us" (II,2). To make this connection was to bridge the distance between novel and romance, explaining, in fact, how his tale "comes under the Romantic definition"(II,2). He was concerned, that is, to reinvent the historical novel, producing not the historical novel of Scott and Cooper, with its carefully dressed characters from another age (the form Hawthorne had used in The Scarlet Letter) which, in its highest development, could show how present modes of thought illuminate the past (as nineteenth century women, for example, inspire a new view of earlier women like Ann Hutchinson through Hester Prynne). This new form of historical novel, however, inverts the earlier model, by showing the present in thrall to the past: contemporary figures shadowed by the giant figures of their ancestors, and continuing a drama begun long ago [7].

The most striking embodiment of inheritance is Judge Pyncheon, who repeats most of the characteristics of his ancestor. In almost every generation of Pyncheons, we are told, one appears who displays such a resemblance to the founder that the gossips whisper "Here is the old Pyncheon come again!" The resemblance between the Judge and the Colonel, whose portrait glowers from the wall of the back parlour, is so remarkable that it seems as if the Colonel had merely to change his dress and lose some weight to become his smaller, hypocritically benign rather than stern, descendant (II,121,122). Phoebe, of course, bears a similar ancestral relation to Alice Pyncheon, and Holgrave

inherits the characteristics of Matthew Maule, but
Clifford is, curiously enough, his own ancestor:
his earlier avatar is the portrait of Clifford as a
young man. He wears the same dressing gown, now
much faded, and displays the same expression; his
imprisonment was a death, so that the Clifford we
see is another version of the early one. Hepzibah
does not have a particular ancestor either: her
model is the house itself. At such points we see
how Hawthorne's method, the saturation of the
narrative by an obsessive idea, can spill over
ordinary categories such as the animate and the
inanimate, the human and the animal, until it
suffuses the whole fictional field; the very hens
and flowers in the backyard are exemplars of the
Pyncheon inheritance, so that house, people and
creatures are intertwined like some suburban House
of Usher which draws all phenomena into its vortex.
This is an extreme version of the paranoid
organisation of the nineteenth century novel, in
which everything is connected to the central spine
as a necessity of form, the imposition of order
upon chaotic experience, making the art of the
novelist an ability to impose coherence (presented
as discovery, or unveiling), on the most disparate
events [8]. The model operates so powerfully that
Holgrave's startling announcement of his identity
in the last chapter does not even elicit a response
from Phoebe, who turns instead to Uncle Venner, to
tell him he must no longer speak of his farm. There
is, in fact, a further connection buried here, in
that Venner, like the Maules, represents the
dispossessed but supposedly equal working class of
America; his needs must also be met in the symbolic
resolution. Nevertheless, Phoebe's indifference to
Holgrave's sinister revelation is strange: we can
only assume that this is an example of irresistible
formal pressure deforming the textual surface; the
inheritance of the novel determining its shape, so
that Holgrave's admission that he is a Maule simply
fills an empty space in the pattern.

The inheritance of genetic characteristics was
becoming the object of scientific scrutiny and
general interest in the first half of the
nineteenth century. In fact Michel Foucault argues,
in a note of obvious relevance to **The House of the
Seven Gables**, that in the nineteenth century there
occured a shift of focus in which concern with
genealogical inheritance, "blood," became a concern
with genetic inheritance:

...many of the themes characteristic of the
caste manners of the nobility reappeared in
the nineteenth century bourgeoisie, but in the
form of biological, medical, or eugenic
precepts. The concern with genealogy became a
preoccupation with heredity; but included in
bourgeois marriages were not only economic
imperatives and rules of social homogeneity,
not only the promises of inheritance, but the
menaces of heredity; families wore and
concealed a sort of reversed and sombre
escutcheon whose defamatory quarters were the
diseases or defects of the group of relatives
[9].

The Pyncheon hereditary illness provides a nice
example of this transition: it changes from a curse
on the family to a genetic defect as the
interpretations of science progress, and in the
same way the wizard's necromantic powers are reread
as mesmerism in the nineteenth century. But in
itself the notion of geneticism is flat: what we
must note is the way in which the idea becomes
impressed upon all available surfaces of the novel.
The Colonel's portrait, for example, which is a
sort of emblem of the dominant Pycheon gene,
contains within itself an impressionistic rendering
of the theme: "In one sense, this picture had
almost faded into the canvass, and hidden itself
behind the duskiness of age; in another, she could
not but fancy that it had been growing more
prominent and strikingly expresssive, ever since
her first familiarity with it, as a child. For,
while the physical outline and substance were
darkening away from the beholder's eye, the bold,
hard, and, at the same time, indirect character of
the man seemed to be brought out in a kind of
spiritual relief." The narrator explains that the
artist's deep conception of his subject's inner
traits is wrought into the picture, and emerges
"after the superficial coloring has been rubbed off
by time" (II,58,59). Hawthorne was always concerned
with the idea of "trace," a general concept of
which inheritance is a specific instance [10]. It
proposes an antinomy between inner and outer in
which the essential nature of the object or event
will emerge through time, however it may be
temporarily disguised. The Judge may differ
superficially from his ancestor, having less meat
on him, and a less stern expression, but he shares
the same deep characteristics; Hepzibah's gaunt
52

skeleton echoes the frame of the house, eaten away
by dry rot; Holgrave had within him the inheritance
of the first wizard, expressed in his name, with
its reference to the early shallow (and now empty?)
grave; Phoebe has the harmony and beauty (if not
the coldness) of Alice Pyncheon; the shrunken hens
carry all the features of their grander
progenitors; and the long dormant seeds planted by
Holgrave produce peculiar scarlet flowering beans,
which bring back the long departed humming birds,
forty years after the last had flowered.
      This saturation of the text by the idea of
inheritance generates a particular kind of
bio-architectural metaphor, in which the self is
seen as a building, containing the inner life (or
death) of the person. Clifford is described as an
occasionally absent guest in the house of his body:
"after a blank moment, there would be a flickering
taper-gleam in his eyeballs. It betokened that his
spiritual part had returned, and was doing its best
to kindle the heart's household fire, and light up
intellectual lamps in the dark and ruinous mansion,
where it was doomed to be a forlorn inhabitant"
(II,105). Hepzibah's brain has been impregnated by
the dry rot of the mansion (II,59), like the house
it has "poor, bare, melancholy chambers" (II,65).
She has the rusty isolation and capacious emptiness
of the house itself, along with its lost potential
for hospitality: her inheritance is sterility, as
the mansion's is emptiness. The Colonel's portrait,
fixed immoveably to the wall of the back parlour,
is a dominant gene in the womb of the house,
overpowering the "miniature" of Clifford, the
recessive inherited taste for luxury and beauty.
Clifford is a sort of aborted possibility of life
for the Pycheon House, his promise of enjoyment and
cultivation thwarted, and perhaps even perverted,
by the dominant strain (II,107). The theme of
renewal thus becomes a matter of the reimpregnation
of the house itself, which is symbolically enacted
late in the novel. But before that the most
elaborate extension of the metaphor comes in a
description of Judge Pyncheon, whose public
position makes him particularly suitable for
visualisation in terms of the social:

      With these materials [gold, landed estate,
      public offices and honours,] and with deeds of
      goodly aspect, done in the public eye, an
      individual of this class builds up, as it
      were, a tall and stately edifice, which, in

the view of other people, and ultimately in his own view, is no other than the man's character, or the man himself. Behold, therefore, a palace! Its splendid halls and suites of spacious apartments are floored with a mosaic-work of costly marbles; its windows, the whole height of each room, admit the sunshine through the most transparent of plate-glass; its high cornices are gilded, and its ceilings gorgeously painted; and a lofty dome - through which, from the central pavement, you may gaze up to the sky, as with no obstructing medium between - surmounts the whole. With what fairer and nobler emblem could any man desire to shadow forth his character? Ah; but in some low and obscure nook - some narrow closet on the ground floor, shut, locked, and bolted, and the key flung away - or beneath the marble pavement, in a stagnant water-puddle, with the richest pattern of mosaic-work above - may lie a corpse, half-decayed, and still decaying, and diffusing its death scent all through the palace! The inhabitant will not be conscious of it; for it has long been his daily breath! Neither will the visitors, for they smell only the rich odors which the master sedulously scatters through the palace, and the incense which they bring, and delight to burn before him! Now and then, perchance, comes a seer, before whose sadly gifted eye the whole structure melts into thin air, leaving only the hidden nook, the bolted closet, with the cobwebs festooned over its forgotten door, or the deadly hole under the pavement, and the decaying corpse within. Here, then, we are to seek the true emblem of the man's character, and of the deed that gives whatever reality it possesses, to his life. And, beneath the show of a marble palace, that pool of stagnant water, foul with many impurities, and perhaps tinged with blood - that secret abomination, above which, possibly, he may say his prayers, without remembering it - is this man's miserable soul! (II,229,230)

The controlling interior pattern, whether it be a rotting corpse, a picture on the wall, or the genetic specification of family traits, amounts to a meta-metaphor in the novel. It is continually imaged, sometimes quite unexpectedly, in almost neurotic repetition. As Jaffrey Pyncheon's crime against Clifford is, in the above illustration, to his elaborately constructed public self, so is Colonel Pyncheon's crime against Matthew Maule a rotting corpse in the House of Pyncheon, and so is the portrait of Colonel Pyncheon to the house, as it ensures that "no good thoughts or purposes could ever spring up and blossom" beneath its evil gaze (II,21). Similarly, we see Jaffrey reenact the image in his own person, as he sits dead within the ancestral mansion, having himself become the corpse at the centre. Matthew Maule's cottage (and his grave?) has the same relation to the Pyncheon "House"; Holgrave has a room within the House of Seven Gables; and all these multiplying instances are versions of the inheritance structure. Once the patterning is perceived, another example of it increases in significance: At the centre of the centre, that is in the space behind the Pyncheon portrait, is a secret opening in the wall containing a document asserting Pyncheon rights to the Eastern territory in Waldo County, which was hidden by Matthew Maule's son Thomas when he built the house.

This central document, the lost legitimation of the Pyncheon claims to wealth, has been made worthless by the passage of time and the establishing of settlers who "would have laughed at the idea of any man's asserting a right – on the strength of mouldy parchments, signed with the faded autographs of governers and legislators, long dead and forgotten – to the lands which they or their fathers had wrested from the wild hand of Nature, by their own sturdy toil!" (II,19) At the very centre of the inheritance structure, then, we find a document which questions the ultimate basis of inheritance, opposing the rights of settlement to the rights of title by legal deed. Where the pattern should be most clearly written, as in the genetic code, there is instead a confusion; the writing turns out to be "hieroglyphics." Yet these are the hieroglyphics of "Indian sagamores" (II,316), rather than "the faded autographs of governors or legislators." Either Hawthorne had forgotten his earlier description, or he wished to revitalise the document through association with aboriginal vitality: a few pages earlier he has arranged for an almost magical accession of wealth to Clifford and Hepzibah; therefore this document may be in some sort a legitimation of the ill-gotten avalanche. The knowledge of the secret
55

spring concealing the manuscript was Holgrave's "only inheritance" from his ancestors (II, 316), so the Maule inheritance is actually the long alienated Pyncheon inheritance: the document so carefully placed in the central position is the final station in a chain of supplementary meanings, it is the supplement itself [11]. But here, not for the first time, nor the last, emerges Hawthorne's ultimate artistic difficulty, on which he eventually foundered: the chain of signifiers is followed ingeniously, one might even say, instinctively, each embodiment examined and discarded in the search for a conclusive version (the portrait in relation to the house; the Judge's crime in relation to his House/body; Maule's cottage in relation to the Pyncheon mansion; Holgrave's room in a wing in relation to the Seven Gables); until at last the narrative arrives at an impasse: here it is at last, the very document itself ... but unreadable and worthless. Its only value lay along the way, in the light that it spilled on to the searchers. Still, there is some speculative meaning to be drawn from the scrap of parchment, perhaps, if we pay a more careful attention to that shift in signatories from colonial to native American autographs.

Not long before writing **The House of the Seven Gables**, Hawthorne had returned to his reading of Rousseau, begun extensively between 1829 and 1832 but now resumed in June and July of 1848 through several withdrawals from the Salem Atheneum [12]. It is reasonable to assume that Hawthorne would have known this passage in **The Social Contract**:

> In general, to establish the right of the first occupier over a plot of ground, the following conditions are necessary: first, the land must not yet be inhabited; secondly, a man must occupy only the amount he needs for his subsistence; and in the third place, possession must be taken, not by an empty ceremony, but by labour and cultivation, the only sign of proprietorship that should be respected by others, in default of a legal title [13].

L.S. Hall notices, in **Hawthorne:Critic of Society** [14], the consonance between these ideas and the statement that the settlers would have laughed at the supposed claims of others to lands which they, or their fathers, had won from nature through toil,
56

if those claims were asserted on the strength of the mere "faded autographs" of governors and legislators. But there is actually a significant reservation in Rousseau's argument: the land must not yet have been inhabited, and the settlers claim is only "in default of a legal title." Do not the original inhabitants, the Indians, have a right to sign away their lands? Is the Pyncheon title more valid, if their hieroglyphs provide a legal title? Buried in the unreadable document is the problem that so exercised Cooper in **The Pioneers**, and later Faulkner in "The Bear": what kinds of rights to the new world may be established, and what is the place of the aboriginal people in any agreement? Rousseau developed his argument to ask, by what right did the Spanish throne claim possession of the whole continent of South America merely on sight? (p.17). By extension, then also, what rights has the present against the past? Settlement is a more powerful argument than a mouldy piece of parchment, and yet the whole of **The House of the Seven Gables** is dedicated to exploring the claims of the past over the present.

From Rousseau, through Jefferson, to Holgrave; the line of influence is clear enough. Holgrave expresses most enthusiastically the right of the present to be free of the past, in Jacksonian diatribes against inheritance resembling the ironic reports in Hawthorne's Notebooks:

> Shall we never, never, get rid of this Past! .... - It lies upon the Present like a giant's dead body! In fact the case is just as if a young giant were compelled to waste all his strength in carrying about the corpse of the old giant, his grandfather, who died a long while ago, and only needs to be decently buried. Just think, a moment; and it will startle you to see what slaves we are to by-gone times - to Death, if we give the matter the right word! ....a Dead man, if he happen to have made a will, disposes of wealth no longer his own; or, if he die intestate, it is distributed in accordance with the notions of men much longer dead than he. A Dead Man sits on all our judgement-seats; and living judges do but search out and repeat his decisions. We read in Dead Men's books! We laugh at Dead Men's jokes, and cry at Dead Men's pathos! We are sick of Dead Men's diseases, physical and moral, and die of the

57

same remedies with which dead doctors killed
their patients! We worship the living Deity,
according to Dead Men's forms and creeds!
Whatever we do, of our own free motion, a Dead
Man's icy hand obstructs us! Turn our eyes to
what point we may, a Dead Man's white,
immitigable face encounters them, and freezes
our very heart! And we must be dead ourselves,
before we can begin to have our proper
influence on the world, which will then be no
longer our world but the world of another
generation, with which we shall have no shadow
of a right to interfere (II,182,183).

Although this may be meant as a humorous burlesque
of the extremes to which Jeffersonian notions had
been taken by Jacksonian enthusiasts, it expresses
in comic terms the dilemmas explored in so much of
Hawthorne's writing. Holgrave has only to add that
a dead man sits within, and disposes emotions
according to dead protocols, to hit off the
ultimate Hawthornean dread. This may be the import
of his idea that "Whatever we seek to do, of our
own free motion, a Dead Man's icy hand obstructs
us," and that "Turn our eyes to what point we may,
a Dead Man's white, immitigable face encounters
them"; statements which are incommensurate with his
political argument but expressive of Holgrave's
personality, inheritance, and position within the
novel. The white, immitigable face anticipates
Holgrave's encounter with Jaffrey's corpse (and
also the puzzle of his extreme reaction to that
encounter); offering a nightmarish perspective from
which both he and the novel need to be rescued by
Phoebe's sublime indifference. "I ought to have
said, too," Holgrave sums up his ravings, "that we
live in Dead Man's houses...." "And why not,"
Phoebe rejoins, "so long as we can be comfortable
in them?" (II,183) According to the narrator,
"these transparent natures are often deceptive in
their depth; those pebbles at the bottom of the
fountain are further from us than we think," and
Phoebe is not to be read like a child's story book
(II,182). Her response is clearly an attempt by
Hawthorne to close off the perspectives of
unrelenting secondariness opened by Holgrave's (as
also Hester's, Coverdale's, Kenyon's or Miriam's)
speculations.

NOTES

1. References in the text are to **The Centenary Edition of the Works of Nathaniel Hawthorne** (Columbus: Ohio State University Press,1965).Vol II.

2. See Sigmund Freud's "Explanations and Applications" in **The Standard Edition of the Complete Works of Sigmund Freud**, London: Hogarth Press, 1964, vol XXII). On repetition in Hawthorne see Eric J. Sundquist, **Home as Found: Authority and Genealogy in Nineteenth Century American Literature** (Baltimore and London: Johns Hopkins University Press, 1979) p. 87., and R.W.B. Lewis, **The American Adam** (1955; Chicago: University of Chicago Press, 1966) p.120.

3. R.W.Emerson, **The Collected Works of Ralph Waldo Emerson**, ed. by R.E. Spiller (Cambridge, Mass: Belknapp Press of Harvard University Press, 1971), p. 24.

4. H.D. Thoreau, **Walden** (New York: Twayne, 1962), p.90.

5. Robert Cantwell, **Nathaniel Hawthorne, The American Years** (New York: Rinehart & Co, 1948) p.397.

6. Orestes Brownson in Perry Miller, ed., **The Transcendentalists** (1950; Cambridge, Mass: Harvard University Press, 1971), p. 437.

7. Space does not permit extended discussion of these issues and Hawthorne's historical tales. See also Georges Lukacs, **The Historical Novel** (London: Merlin, 1962).

8. Leo Bersani, **A Future for Astyanax** (Boston: Little, Brown & Co, 1976).

9. Michel Foucault, **The History of Sexuality, Volume One** (La Volonte de Savoire, 1976); tr. Robert Hurley (Harmondsworth: Penguin Books, 1981) pp.124, 125.

10. See "Footprints in Sand," below, and my earlier discussion of trace in **The Scarlet Letter**.

11. On the supplement, see "The Elaborated Sign," above.

12. Marion Kesselring, **Hawthorne's Reading** (Folcroft, Pa: Folcroft Press, 1969) p. 60.

13. Jean Jacques Rousseau, **The Social Contract, and Discourses** ed. G.D.H. Cole (London: Dent, 1955) p.17.

14. L.S. Hall, **Hawthorne: Critic of Society** (1944; Gloucester, Mass: Peter Smith, 1966) p. 162.

4 THE DEPLOYMENT OF SEXUALITY

The pressure of the past on the present in **The House of the Seven Gables** is felt most acutely through the institution of the family, as Holgrave insists. "Under that roof, through a portion of three centuries, there has been perpetual remorse of conscience, a constantly defeated hope, strife amongst kindred, various misery, a strange form of death, dark suspicion, unspeakable disgrace, - all, or most of which calamity, I have the means of tracing to the old Puritan's inordinate desire to plant and endow a family. To plant a family! This idea is at the bottom of most of the wrong and mischief which men do!" (II,185). The formation of a structure of personal relations based on alliance is antithetical to the democratic and egalitarian ideas espoused by Holgrave, and to the new American ethos generally. So Holgrave sees the House of Pyncheon as an anachronism, which is, moreover, infected with lunacy through its inbreeding propensities. "Human blood," he claims,"in order to keep its freshness, should run in hidden streams, as the water of an aqueduct is conveyed in subterranean pipes" (II,185). Yet although Holgrave's levelling political thought combines with his biologism in hostility to "family," he is, as we soon see, about to embark upon the planting of a family of his own, with Phoebe. Rather than accept this as a simple irony, in which the erstwhile reformer is won over by the pleasures of bed and board, I wish to propose it as an expression of the place of Holgrave and Phoebe in the novel as representatives of "sexuality," as opposed to "alliance," which is represented by Hepzibah and Clifford.

The terms are taken from Michel Foucault's

History of Sexuality, in which he argues that one
of the major changes in sexuality over the three
centuries mentioned by Holgrave was a shift from
alliance to sexuality. In every society, he says,
the relations of sex had given rise to a system "of
marriage, of fixation and development of kinship
ties, of transmission of names and possessions"
[1]. But this "deployment of alliance," with its
complex mechanisms of constraint and knowledge,
lost importance from the eighteenth century onwards
in new political and economic structures, and
without being completely supplanted, lost ground to
"a new apparatus which was superimposed upon the
previous one": the deployment of sexuality. Like
the alliance system, this "connects up with the
circuit of sexual partners," but in a different
way:

> The deployment of alliance is built around a
> system of rules defining the permitted and the
> forbidden, the licit and the illicit, whereas
> the deployment of sexuality operates according
> to mobile, polymorphous, and contingent
> techniques of power. The deployment of
> alliance has as one of its chief objectives to
> reproduce the interplay of relations and
> maintain the law that sustains them; the
> deployment of sexuality, on the other hand,
> engenders a continual extension of areas and
> forms of control ... if the deployment of
> alliance is firmly tied to the economy due to
> the role it can play in the transmission or
> circulation of wealth, the deployment of
> sexuality is linked to the economy through
> numerous and subtle relays, the main one of
> which, however, is the body - the body that
> produces and consumes. In a word, the
> deployment of alliance is attuned to a
> homeostasis of the social body, which it has
> the function of maintaining; whence its
> priviliged link with the law; whence too the
> fact that the important phrase for it is
> "reproduction." The deployment of sexuality
> has its reason for being, not in reproducing
> itself, but in proliferating, innovating,
> annexing, creating, and penetrating bodies in
> an increasingly detailed way, and controlling
> populations in an increasingly comprehensive
> way (pp.106,107).

Foucault does not suggest that sexuality replaced

alliance in this period; in fact he stresses that
it was on the basis of alliance that the deployment
of sexuality was constructed. This explains the
emergence of the sexuality embodied in Phoebe and
Holgrave, out of the alliance structure of the
"Family" and its ancestral home. When sexual
attraction had previously occurred, in
contravention of the alliance structure, as when
Alice Pyncheon was attracted to Matthew Maule in
the story Holgrave tells to express his sense of
the family's history (and as a seduction device),
the result was a catastrophic defeat for the
deployment of sexuality: Alice, so enmeshed within
the alliance structure as to be unconscious of her
sexual admiration for the handsome carpenter, opens
herself to his domination through the pride that is
unwilling to admit equality; the enclosing alliance
structure forbids any other possibility than her
humiliation by Maule and consequent death.

But at the time in which **The House of the
Seven Gables** is set, the deployment of alliance is
displayed at the point of breakdown: the Judge, who
is the principal male representative of the House,
is excluded from the family mansion, which is
occupied by Hepzibah, the sterile product of
degeneration due to inbreeding (like the hens), and
Clifford, the once beautiful, impotent male whose
absence of energy suggests the end of the
cloistered alliance structure. It is, perhaps,
easier for most readers to accept that Clifford,
Hepzibah and the Judge represent the decadent end
of the traditional family structure of alliance
than it is to agree that Holgrave and Phoebe
represent the beginning of a new form of regulation
of sexual relations worthy of the name "the
deployment of sexuality." Most critics have
insisted that Phoebe is as removed from sexuality
as possible, and Holgrave does not appear as a man
of passion. But the movement from alliance to
sexuality is not a Lawrentian unleashing of sensual
indulgence and passionate love; it is a way of
describing a different ordering of sexual relations
which replaces the hierarchical dispositions
according to family interrelationships by a new set
of determinants, of which the freedom of Holgrave
and Phoebe to dispose of themselves as they choose,
according to personal attraction, is illustrative.
Nor is Phoebe, in fact, desexualised by the novel:
on the contrary, the descriptions of the young girl
are imbued with a Victorian prurience, which
increases in sexual force through its overt denials

63

Eve Tempted

of sexual reference; just as, Foucault notes, the
Victorians learned to multiply discussions of
sexuality, while appearing to repress them
[p.22,23].

In **The Blithedale Romance** the phenomena of
mesmeric fascination are brought into the discourse
of sexuality almost automatically: the account
given by the man in blue spectacles immediately
focuses on this aspect of the pseudo-science.
Similarly, in **The House of the Seven Gables** the
effects of magetism are described in terms of
sado-masochistic sexual surrender: Phoebe ready for
seduction; the artist conscious of his power:

> With the lids drooping over her eyes – now
> lifted, for an instant, and drawn down again,
> as with leaden weights – she leaned slightly
> towards him, and seemed almost to regulate her
> breath by his.... A veil was beginning to be
> muffled about her, in which she could behold
> only him, and live only in his thoughts and
> emotions. His glance, as he fastened it on the
> young girl, grew involuntarily more
> concentrated; in his attitude, there was the
> consciousness of power, investing his hardly
> mature figure with a dignity that did not
> belong to its physical manifestation (II,211).

Nor is Phoebe's everyday domestic presence divested
of sexuality by the narration: in fact she stirs
sexual desire in the Judge and even, impossible as
it seems, in the decrepit Clifford. In describing
the relationship between Clifford and Phoebe the
narrator is at pains to acknowledge the exact
shading of prurient connotation:

> ...his sentiment for Phoebe, without being
> paternal, was not the less chaste than if she
> had been his daughter. He was a man, it is
> true, and recognised her as a woman. She was
> his only representative of womankind. He took
> unfailing note of every charm that appertained
> to her sex, and saw the ripeness of her lips,
> and the virginal development of her bosom. All
> her little, womanly ways, budding out of her
> like blossoms on a young fruit tree, had their
> effect on him, and sometimes caused his very
> heart to tingle with the keenest thrills of
> pleasure (II,141).

At any rate Phoebe soon felt that, if not the
profound insight of a seer, yet a more than

64

feminine delicacy of appreciation was making
her the subject of its regard. A moment
before, she had known nothing which she would
have sought to hide. Now, as if some secret
were hinted to her consciousness through the
medium of another's perception, she was fain
to let her eyelids droop beneath Clifford's
gaze. A blush, too - the redder, because she
strove hard to keep it down - ascended higher
and higher, in a tide of fitful progress,
until even her brow was all suffused with it
(II,220).

One almost expects Clifford to burst forth with
some Lovelacean remark about the "little charmer";
instead he offers the more restrained flower
analogy favoured by the narrator: "Girlhood has
passed into womanhood; the bud is a bloom"
(II,220). It is not, perhaps, entirely the matter
of Phoebe's being in love that is hinted to her, so
much as her sexual maturity.

I note these points at some length because
even readers like Frederic Crews, who might have
been expected to admit them, have instead tended to
emphasize Phoebe's lack of sexuality. Crews
declares that "Phoebe's chief part in the romance
... is not simply to stand for innocence but to
refute or 'exorcise' sexual cynicism ... Hawthorne
deliberately puts her within a sexual perspective
in order to declare her exempt from erotic
inclinations" [2]. It is rather that the erotic
fascination is increased (for Hawthorne's
contemporaries) by the association with innocence,
girlhood, and domesticity. Clifford, Hawthorne, and
the reader, are being given license to examine
Phoebe and enjoy her body, as Clifford does above,
without compromising themselves by the
acknowledgment of these forbidden impulses.

As first among the relays through which the
deployment of sexuality is linked to the economy
Foucault stresses "the body that produces and
consumes" [p.107] [3], and it would not be amiss to
consider this aspect of Phoebe also. "There is
little question," says Foucault, "that one of the
primordial forms of class consciousness is the
affirmation of the body; at least, this was the
case for the bourgeoisie during the eighteenth
century. It converted the blue blood of the nobles
into a sound organism and a healthy sexuality"
[p.126]. This was doubtless even more true of

America's ostensibly anti-aristocratic society than
of European cultures. Phoebe is the sun, the
life-giver, a young <u>fruit</u> tree; she is also, in
abeyance of her reproductive functions, a provider
of gastronomic delights. When she arrives at the
House of Seven Gables she immediately makes herself
indispensable by the production of delicious food.
Eating is used throughout the novel as one of the
measures of sensuality, from the legendary
grossness of the first meal in the house, with its
capacious hearths for cooking, to the animal
appetite of Judge Jaffrey and the crude "voracity"
of Clifford's hunger, which (like his sexuality)
makes Phoebe "drop her eyes" (II,107). The little
boy, Ned Higgins, with his prodigious capacity for
gingerbread creatures, is one of the running
comedies of the book, tepid on the surface perhaps,
but filled with subtle implication. Hepzibah's
productions in this line tend to dismemberment: the
elephant loses three legs and a trunk; the "Jim
Crow" has a broken foot, becoming "bits of musty
gingerbread" (II,37); whereas the active Phoebe,
contrastingly, is able to bake little cakes which
"whosoever tasted, would longingly desire to taste
again" (II,79). Throughout the novel Phoebe
satisfies the cannibalistic inclinations of the boy
in a relationship which seems to exemplify the
relations between the shop, the house and its
inhabitants, and the street or outside world.

        The shop and its young assistant, together
with the customers and their needs, could be
regarded as as a glossary of Foucault's main
elements of the deployment of sexuality: "the
feminine body, infantile precocity, the regulation
of births, and, to a lesser extent, no doubt, the
specification of the perverted" [p.108]. The
opening of the shop provides a metaphor for the
institution of sexuality rather than alliance in
the fortunes of the Pyncheon family. As with the
precedent for Holgrave and Phoebe given by Alice
and Matthew, the experiment has been tried, and
failed, before. This time it succeeds, in a sense.
"Pretty good business," as the sagacious Dixey says
at the end. The shop is the place of intercourse
between the house, so long sealed up, and the
world. One of the least attractive features of
Hawthorne's comedy at Hepzibah's expense is this
buried analogy between the shop and the old woman's
sexuality. The narrator comments archly that "the
matter is disagreeably delicate to handle" (II,28).
This unused shop, in which Hepzibah and her brother
66

played as children, is overswept by the foliage of
the elm and concealed beneath an impending gable;
it has a corridor to the womblike interior of the
house with a door between, on which Hawthorne makes
some cryptic play after the climactic penetration
and death of Judge Jaffrey. The inner door was
closed (II,290), but soon "not closed, as the child
had seen it, but ajar, and almost wide open"
(II,292); which appears to be completely redundant
information except in terms of the house - as -
body paradigm. In making herself mistress of the
shop, then, Phoebe is covertly signalled as
establishing a new regime of sexuality.

Phoebe's entrance to the house is
(appropriately) not via the shop door, but by means
of the main entrance. Holgrave too, has his own
means of access to the house, although we do see
him use the shop entrance once, when Hepzibah is
opening it on his advice. The Judge, however, uses
the shop in his attempt to force an entrance, after
trying to kiss Phoebe: "The man, the sex, somehow
or other, was entirely too prominent in the Judge's
demonstrations of that sort," which causes Phoebe's
eyes to sink and her face to blush, as we would
expect (II,118). He thrusts her aside in his
determination to enter, but barring the way to the
inner chamber (where he is indeed "at home," as he
says, for the portrait hangs there, signalling his
genetic dominance) he encounters Hepzibah, "a
perfect picture of prohibition, at full length, in
the dark frame of the doorway"(II,127). The object
of this mock rape is Clifford, who cries out: "go
down on your knees to him! Kiss his feet! Entreat
him not to come in! Oh, let him have mercy on me!
Mercy! - mercy!" thus interrupting the Judge's
"evident purpose of forcing a passage," as he steps
forward with a "certain hot fellness of purpose,
which annihilated everything but itself" (II,129).
One of the books that Phoebe reads to Clifford is,
of course, **The Rape of the Lock**, but there may be a
serious undertone in this tasteless comedy: at
issue is whether the House of Pyncheon will
continue in its claustrophobic alliance mould, or
if it will be reinvigorated by the Pyncheon - Maule
alliance long forbidden by ancestral pride and
guilt. The inner chamber contains the dominant
strain of the Pyncheon genetic inheritance,
emblematised in the Colonel's portrait, which quite
overshadows the recessive strain similarly
symbolised in Clifford's Malbone miniature. Lest
this be thought rather anachronistic, I should

Eve Tempted

point out that such information was just becoming
available: "In the same period, the analysis of
heredity was placing sex (sexual relations,
venereal diseases, matrimonial alliances,
perversions) in a position of 'biological
responsibility' with regard to the species: not
only could sex be affected by its own diseases, it
could also, if it was not controlled, transmit
diseases or create others that would afflict future
generations" [Foucault, p. 118]. Judge Jaffrey
hopes that his meeting with Clifford, here
specified as a sort of rape, will result in a new
fruitfulness for the family fortunes, when Clifford
reveals his secret. But the Pyncheon bull, after
finally achieving penetration of the inner chamber
and taking his rightful place in the ancestral
chair, succumbs to the hereditary disease and dies
with his plans unconsummated.

Much ingenuity has been exercised by critics who
hope to establish more clearly the motivation of
this convenient, but apparently accidental, death.
Why should the Judge die now, and not at an earlier
point, or after he has sent Clifford to the Asylum?
Crews, for example, believes Jaffrey to be a victim
of shock: he sees Clifford, but assumes he is the
ghost of his Uncle Clifford, whose death he
exploited. "A Clifford, in this event, has caused
the death of Jaffrey after Jaffrey has caused the
death of a Clifford" [4]. Unfortunately for the
elegance of this theory the Uncle's name was
actually Jaffrey. The point remains that readers
seek some sort of reasonable causation for such a
central event in the plot as this one, which, along
with the death of the Judge's only son, reverses
the direction of the novel. But in Hawthorne's
expressionist interiors events may sometimes have
only an imaginative adequation: the Judge's death
is a corollary of the new sexual circuit between
Holgrave and Phoebe, whose love began in the Edenic
garden and is consummated (not literally, of
course) in the empty room which had formerly been
the grand reception room of the mansion, rather
than the dismal back parlour. Here the "flower of
Eden" blooms again; the deployment of sexuality
usurps the deployment of alliance (although it
grows out of it, as the flower of Eden grows out of
the old earth):

 Neither was he in haste, like her, to betake
 himself within the precincts of common life.
 On he contrary, he gathered a wild enjoyment -

68

as it were, a flower of strange beauty, growing in a desolate spot, and blossoming in the wind - such a flower of momentary happiness he gathered from his present position. It separated Phoebe and himself from the world, and bound them to each other, by their exclusive knowledge of Judge Pyncheon's mysterious death, and the counsel they were forced to keep respecting it ... The image of awful Death, whch filled the house, held them united by his stiffened grasp. These influences hastened the development of emotions, that might not otherwise have flowered so soon. Possibly, indeed, it had been Holgrave's purpose to let them die in their undeveloped germs (II,305).

Shortly afterwards, however, Holgrave announces his presentiment that it will soon be his lot to "set out trees, to make fences - perhaps, even, in due time, to build a house for another generation..." (II,307). He intends to plant a family: is this not the reinstitution of alliance?

The answer to that question illuminates much of Hawthorne's writing, besides The House of the Seven Gables. According to Foucault "the family, in its contemporary form [that is, since the eighteenth century] must not be understood as a social, economic, and political structure of alliance that excludes, or at least restrains sexuality, that diminishes it as much as possible, preserving only its useful function. On the contrary, its role is to anchor sexuality and provide it with a permanent support" [p.108]. Holgrave's acceptance of the family structure is not then necessarily an adoption of the forms of alliance. We might usefully compare it to Hathorne's own marriage, which by no means united the Peabody and Hawthorne families but rather established itself in terms of opposition to these, in terms of its own sexuality. "The family is the interchange of sexuality and alliance," says Foucault: it conveys the law and the juridical dimension in the deployment of sexuality; and it conveys the economy of pleasure and the intensity of sensations in the regime of alliance" (p.108). But this means that the sexuality of the family is incestuous: "Since the eighteenth century the family has become an obligatory locus of affects, feelings, love"; therefore sexuality "has its privileged point of development in the family" and is "incestuous" from

69

the start [pp.108,109]. "In a society such as ours, where the family is the most active site of sexuality [incest] occupies a central place; it is constantly being solicited and refused; it is an object of obsession and attraction, a dreadful secret and an indispensable pivot" [p.109]. The relations between the Pyncheons are incestuous, as the model of the inbred hens demonstrates, and Clifford and Hepzibah particularly are presented in this way. The love between Phoebe and Holgrave is not incestuous - until we reflect on the intimacy of the hereditary tie between them; their sibling-like situation as residents of the same house; and the nature of their semi-filial, semi-paternal relationship to Hepzibah and Clifford, the parents in the fantasy family. But it is not important to discover whether there is an incestuous twist in their love, the point of interest here is the notion of incest as "the object of obsession and attraction, a dreadful secret and indispensable pivot in the family." Many attempts to account for the suggestions of incest in Hawthorne's fiction have foundered upon the need to psychoanalyse the inacessible writer, or posit an unprovable family history for him, without understanding that it is a cultural question necessarily encountered in analysing the family, as Hawthorne does here, or even civilization itself, as he does in **The Marble Faun.**

The House of the Seven Gables deals with large issues, as do all of Hawthorne's novels, presented within a domestic but expressionist context, and investigating the "springs and motive secrets" (II, 73) of human behaviour. The great issue in this novel is whether all are doomed to follow out the same mechanical actions, like the puppet figures on the Italian's barrel organ, created perhaps by some cynic, who "had desired to signify in this pantomimic scene [including a lover's kiss] that we mortals, whatever our business or amusement ... all dance to one identical tune, and, in spite of our ridiculous activity, bring nothing finally to pass. For the most remarkable aspect of the affair was, that, at the cessation of the music, everybody was petrified at once, from the most extravagent life into a dead torpor" (II,163). The only figure which remains moving after this show is the mean and low, prying and crafty, insatiable monkey, with his obscene phallic tail, who represents the "grossest form of the love of money" (II,164). In attempting to posit a counterforce of renewal, which could "transfigure the earth and make it Eden again," and overcome the "heavy earth-dream" (II,307), Hawthorne began to investigate the relation of the family to the structures of power, and developed a contrast between the legitimations of alliance and the transmutation of these into sexuality. Elaborate patterns of correspondencies express the introverted decay of the alliance structure, which can only be evaded or exorcised by a renegotiation of the nature of "family", opening the closed doors of dynastic wealth and privilege to despised outgroups such as the Maules and the Venners. The evident hollowness of this as an answer to large scale economic exploitation does not diminish its imaginative force as justification of Hawthorne's politically temporising position in his attempted mediation between democratic theory and oligarchic fact, without recourse to violent solutions.

Whether social renewal might be possible without violence was also the question behind **The Blithedale Romance** (1852). Here Hawthorne decribed the attempts of New England reformers, himself among them, to develop new forms of relationship between the sexes, supplanting "family," and between the community and the larger society; to reinvent Eden in agrarian simplicity.

NOTES

1. This and subsequent references are to Michel Foucault, **The History of Sexuality**, vol 1, tr. Robert Hurley (Harmondsworth: Penguin Books, 1981), p.106. More specifically American aspects of these changes may be seen in G.J. Barker-Benfield, **The Horrors of the Half-Known Life: Male attitudes to Women and Sexuality in Nineteenth Century America** (New York: Harper Colophon, 1976).

2. Frederick Crews, **The Sins of the Fathers** (New York: Oxford University Press, 1966) p. 186.

3. "One of [the bourgeoisie's] primary concerns was to provide itself with a body and a sexuality - to ensure the strength, endurance, and secular proliferation of that body through the organization of a deployment of sexuality." (Foucault, pp. 125,126).

4. Crews, **The Sins of the Fathers**, p.177. See also Alfred H. Marks, "Who Killed Judge Pyncheon? The Role of the Imagination in **The House of the Seven Gables**" PMLA LXXI (June, 1956) pp. 355-369.

5 THE FOURTH SIDE: THE BLITHEDALE ROMANCE

The fourth side borrows a term from theatre, to describe the openness of the stage from the perspective of the audience (and also the director, and writer). **The Blithedale Romance** draws heavily on the theatrical metaphor and thereby insists of any analysis that it take fully into account the reception aesthetic which is built into the text. The fourth side is also a term used in Jacques Derrida's acerbic criticism of Lacan's celebrated "Seminar on the Purloined Letter." Derrida points out that Poe's story cannot be regarded simply in terms of triangular scenes, as Lacan would have it, because the "general narrator" also makes significant comments. Lacan describes how the participants in the triangular situation in turn each imagine themselves to be unseen while seeing: "The third sees that the first two glances leave what should be hidden exposed to whoever would seize it: the minister, and finally Dupin.... Three partners: the second believing itself invisible because the first has its head stuck in the ground, and all the while letting the third calmly pluck its rear" [1]. At the end, Dupin is said to break off his temporary identification with the minister, so withdrawing from the circuit - which for Lacan is a circuit of adequation involving restitution of the letter to its proper place in return for a sort of spending of wealth - leaving Dupin as the only one who sees everything. There is no need here to investigate the complexities of Derrida's attack upon the analyst for taking up the role of Dupin and imagining that he, unseen, sees everything, or believing that he is returning the "letter" of Freud's teaching to the master, out of the hands of

73

Eve Tempted

"cooks" like Marie Bonaparte [2]. What I wish to adopt is the strategic recognition of the fourth side, as the textual frame which enables writer and reader to stand back and see. In **The Blithedale Romance** Miles Coverdale provides that fourth side, being writer and reader as well as participant in the dramatic action he describes, of which the other three sides are constituted by the perceptual positions of Zenobia, Hollingsworth, and Priscilla [3].

In the text, to follow up Lacan's metaphor, Priscilla sees nothing, being beneath the veil; Hollingsworth sees only his own scheme, that is, himself; Zenobia sees Hollingsworth and Priscilla; but none of them really see Coverdale, who sees all of them. Hence the fourth side. But we, the readers, are included in this fourth side, along with the effaced author. The distances thus established are worth notice: what little action there is takes place between Priscilla, Hollingsworth and Zenobia; it is observed by Coverdale, who writes of it many years later, to be read by us, the audience of readers. The use of a narrator who is both in and out of the game is not in itself exceptional, but it becomes so when the subject of the text is precisely that distance between the narrator and experience, his voyeurism or, in other words, the supplement:

> The supplement will always be the moving of the tongue or acting through the hands of others. In it everything is brought together: progress as the possibility of perversion, regression towards an evil that is not natural and that adheres to the power of substitution that permits us to absent ourselves and act by proxy, through representation, through the hands of others. Through the written. This substitution always has the form of the sign. The scandal is that the sign, the image, or the representer, become forces and "make the world move" [4].

In using the term voyeurism a certain moral disapprobation is implied which is avoided when we consider the inescapability of supplementarity in language, whether written or spoken, symbolic perception; or even "nature" [5]. It may be thought that Derrida's "scandal" implies disapprobation from the vantage of an essentialist metaphysic denied by his own discourse. But it is exactly that

74

insecurity that is described as scandalous, in
contrast to the complacency with which we readers
(voyeurs) accuse Coverdale of our own disposition
[6]. Which ostrich does one wish to be?

The meta-realism which includes the writer and
the reader within the text constitutes a diminution
of the "realism" of the novel while aspiring to
another, perhaps more fundamental, version of the
real. For a nineteenth century novel **The Blithedale
Romance** displays a high level of negativity [7],
like Melville's **The Confidence Man** or Poe's
Narrative of Arthur Gordon Pym, which forces the
reader to confront his own assumptions as these are
held up in an ironic mirroring: "I - I myself - was
in love - with - Priscilla," stammers poor
Coverdale (III,247), which is only what the reader
would expect, <u>then</u> ("Reader, I married him!"),
although not <u>now,</u> when readers would prefer to have
him fixated on Zenobia, the more "real" woman [8].
What either reading fails to see is that Coverdale
is more interested in the etiology of "love" than
its validity. He says of Priscilla, "if any mortal
really cares for her it is myself, and not even I,
for her realities - poor little seamstress, as
Zenobia rightly called her! - but for the fancy
work with which I have idly decked her out"
(III,100). And of Zenobia, the converse may be
said: it is the fancy work with which Coverdale
<u>strips</u> her that constitutes her attraction: "...a
silken kerchief, between which and her gown there
was one glimpse of a white shoulder. It struck me
as a great piece of good fortune that there should
be just that glimpse" (III,15). In another instance
Coverdale says, "...the fault must have been
entirely in my imagination -but these last words,
together with something in her manner, irresistibly
brought up a picture of that fine, perfectly
developed figure, in Eve's earliest garment"
(III,17). So "love", the engine of the conventional
novel, and eroticism, its driver, are subjected to
an interrogation that includes the reader, while
pretending only to criticise Coverdale. But the
text goes further: it investigates the role of the
sign or representer in the creation of the
supplement by further displacements of eroticism
into Priscilla's veil and silk purses, and the
hothouse flowers in Zenobia's hair.

Zenobia is introduced, in the above scene,
wearing a single flower in her glossy hair. "It was
an exotic, of rare beauty, and as fresh as if the
hot-house gardener had just clipt it from the stem"

Eve Tempted

(III,15). As if to syphon off some of the dangerous
symbolic fragrance of this bloom Coverdale is quick
to moralize it: "That flower has struck deep root
into my memory. I can both see it and smell it, at
this moment. So brilliant, so rare, so costly as it
must have been, and yet enduring only for a day, it
was more indicative of the pride and pomp, which
had a luxuriant growth in Zenobia's character, than
if a great diamond had sparkled among her hair"
(III,15). As with Miriam's ruby-like secret in The
Marble Faun the sexual significance of this flower
is immediately apparent, reinforced by Coverdale's
intuition that the flower is a talisman (III,45),
which, as long as he continued to know her,
affected his imagination as "a subtle expression"
of her character. This meditation on the flower
culminates in his obsessive perception: "Zenobia is
a wife! Zenobia has lived, and loved! There is no
folded petal, no latent dew-drop, in this perfectly
developed rose!"(III,47). The transmutation of
Zenobia's flower from hot-house bloom to the
artificial replica flower that she wears in the
town – "her characteristic flower, though it seemed
to be still there, had undergone a cold and bright
transfiguration; it was a flower exquisitely
imitated in jeweller's work, and imparting the last
touch that transformed Zenobia into a work of
art"(III,164) – begins to bear out Coverdale's
desire that Zenobia should sit endlessly to
sculptors "because the cold decorum of the marble
would consist with the utmost scantiness of
drapery" (III,44), and also anticipates the
repellent rigidification that occurs in her dead
body. But more than this, it registers Coverdale's
own petrification of eroticism and investment in
the supplement which, like Owen Warland's in "The
Artist of the Beautiful," or Kenyon's in The Marble
Faun, is located in the very object of desire
itself: sexuality, in Coverdale's response to
Zenobia, is initially exotic, a hot-house flower,
and subsequently lapidary, a jewelled simalcrum of
desirability.

Priscilla's purses, on the other hand, are
exemplary of reticence: their "peculiar excellence,
besides the great delicacy and beauty of the
manufacture, lay in the almost impossibility that
any uninitiated person should discover the
aperture; although, to a practised touch, they
would open as wide as charity or prodigality might
wish. I wondered," Coverdale continues," if it were
not a symbol of Priscilla's own mystery" (III,35).
76

He has seen such purses before, and claims to be, in fact, the possessor of one (III,35), which might be read as a reference to his own virginity or, more ambiguously, his own experience as a "deflowerer" of virgins. My intention here is not to rediscover familiar sexual tokens but to point to the <u>process</u> by which the supposedly vital and erotic is subjected to the signifier, the image or representer or, more exactly, is only enabled to appear <u>through</u> that subjection. As with the example of Zenobia's shoulder (compare Barthe's "where the cloth gapes," or her nakedness (in "Eve's earliest garment") [9], the erotic appears only in its substitutions or even, in Priscilla, its denials. Thus Priscilla's veil begins to take on a larger significance.

The veil itself appears physically on two occasions: when Zenobia flings a piece of gauzy fabric over Priscilla while telling the story of Theodore; and when Priscilla appears on stage with Westervelt. In both appearances the import of the veil is "mystery"; the origins of Priscilla, the identity of the Veiled Lady. This mystery is eroticised in Zenobia's story of Theodore who is asked to kiss a hidden face before uncovering it, but refuses to do so. Rumour has it that the face is beautiful, but also that it may be hideous: the face of a corpse, a skeleton, a "monstrous visage, with snaky locks, like Medusa's, and one great red eye in the centre of the forehead" (III,110). In the event, the face that Theodore pruriently uncovers does not display "the grinning cavities of a monster's mouth" (III,113), but is instead a" pale, lovely face" which soon disappears, only to haunt him for the rest of his life. So the Medusa promise is obliquely fulfilled as Theodore is petrified into a rigid posture of devotion to the unattainable, and a reverence for the sacredness that he profaned. This parable anticipates Coverdale's own experience for he, like Theodore, chooses the distance of his perspective and is then condemned to keep it. It also bears directly on the identity of Priscilla, which Zenobia reveals by the action of reconcealing her. Her identity is, firstly, the Veiled Lady of the exhibition halls, and Old Moodie's daughter, Zenobia's step sister; but secondly, the <u>inconnue</u>, whose identity consists in her unknowability, an absence projected as presence, like the category "virgin." She is, in other words, the supplement itself, and from this derives her erotic power over Coverdale and even

Hollingsworth.

The exhibition of the Veiled Lady attended by both men in "A Village Hall" proposes a further refinement: the Veiled Lady is infinitely passive, responsive to the slightest instruction or even gesture of her mesmeriser, yet she is also infinitely indifferent; she cannot be made aware of the audience, no matter what movements or noises they make. Only Hollingsworth is able to penetrate this magnetic cocoon, through the "power of his great, stern, yet tender soul" (III,203), and here too her response is simply to hand over control from Westervelt to Hollingsworth. The hymeneal veil is an impenetrability, which opens to the husband figure while allowing sexual titillation to the cold gaze of the audience: "She threw off the veil, and stood before that multitude of people, pale, tremulous, shrinking, as if only then had she discovered that a thousand eyes were gazing at her" (III,203).

Such acts of concealment and public exposure, which have their echoes throughout Hawthorne's fiction: in Hester and Dimmesdale on the scaffold platform; Miriam at the Piazza of the Porta del Populo; and the Reverend Hooper's taking the veil; all obviously carry significance beyond their immediate meanings. Like Zenobia's shadowy outline upon the white curtain of her drawing room the veil presents a kind of hieroglyphic which challenges all decipherment (III,162) [10]. In the Preface to **The Marble Faun** Hawthorne announced his intention to make his "most reverential bow, and retire behind the curtain," given that his ideal reader was by now probably "under some mossy grave-stone, inscribed with a half-obliterated name, which I shall never recognise" (IV, Preface). This recapitulates a comment he made in "The Old Manse": "So far as I am a man of really individual attributes, I veil my face..." (X,33), and another remark, in his Introduction to **The Scarlet Letter**, that if we imagine that a kind and apprehensive friend (though not the closest) is listening, "we may prate of the circumstances that lie around us, and even of ourself, but still keep the inmost Me behind its veil" (I,3,4). Priscilla's veil, then, may have a connection with the frequent but limited self revelations offered by the author, which John Irwin has described as "not a drawing back of the veil, but an imprinting on the veil's surface of what lies 'behind' it, a pictographic cypher addressed to "the few who will understand him"
78

[11]. But more than self revelation, I believe, the
veil in **The Blithedale Romance** problematises the
very basis of the self and its desires.

The veil comes between the presumed real self
and the presumed real world, preventing the two
from contact and thus, for example, insulating a
nun from evil. In Coverdale's development of that
metaphor, within the veil flung over her by "an
evil hand", Westervelt's, but also, we notice,
Zenobia's, Priscilla keeps inviolate "her virgin
reserve and sanctity of soul" through all the
"jugglery that had hitherto environed her"
(III,203). The saving veil is itself part of the
"jugglery"; in other words, Priscilla is untouched
by her own actions and experience, because the real
Priscilla is somehow other. Anagrammatically, evil
becomes veil.

But the veil remains ominous, in a way that
emerges through examination of a book that greatly
impressed Hawthorne, Rousseau's **Julie, ou La
Nouvelle Heloise** [12]. Visiting Clarens in 1859,
Hawthorne was reminded of the effect of Rousseau's
novel on his youthful imagination: "Clarens... has
still another interest for me; for I found myself
more affected by it, as the scene of the love of
St. Preux and Julia, than I have often been by
scenes of poetry and romance" [13]. The metaphor of
the veil dominates the latter part of **La Nouvelle
Heloise**, after the letter in which St Preux
describes his recurrent dream of Julie taking the
place of her mother on her death bed:

> She could not finish....I tried to raise my
> eyes and look at her; I saw her no more. In
> her face I saw Julie. I saw her; I recognised
> her although her face was covered with a veil.
> I gave a shriek, I rushed forward to put aside
> the veil, I could not reach it. I stretched
> forth my arms, I tormented myself, but I
> touched nothing. "Friend, be calm," she said
> to me in a faint voice." "The terrible veil
> covers me. No hand can put it aside." (Letter
> IX, Part V, p.365)

What is this veil? First, it is a prefiguration of
her death, soon to occur. In this context the dream
serves as an omen, as it is registered by her
friend Madame d'Orbe, who writes: "Since I received
your fatal letter...I do not come near Julie
without trembling over losing her. At every moment
I think I see the pallor of death on her face, and

this morning, pressing her in my arms, I felt myself in tears without knowing why. That veil! That veil! ...There is something indefinably sinister in it which disturbs me each time I think of it" (Letter X, Part V, p.369). After Julie's death Madame d'Orbe again refers to "the veil", without further explanation (Letter X, Part VI, p.396). Another implication is of course religious: Julie has, in a sense, "taken the veil" in choosing heavenly over earthly happiness. But a subtler connotation is of the illusion of love that Julie has apparently been at such pains to demystify, for **La Nouvelle Heloise** is a sentimental novel which turns back upon itself and deconstructs the idea on which it has depended. After Julie's letter performs the shift from love to friendship (or pretends to do so), and calmly registers the fact of her happy marriage to Wolmar (Letter XVIII, Part III, pp. 254-256), the reader is forced to reconsider all that previously seemed to be the obstacles to the passionate love between Julie and St Preux. As Paul de Man describes this peripeteia: "there is not a single episode, practically not a single word, in the more than hundred letters that come before the turning point that is not clarified and accounted for by the redoubled reading that the reversal compels us to undertake. In the place of 'love', based on the resemblances and substitutions of body and soul or self and other, appears the contractual agreement of marriage, set up as a defence against the passions and as the basis of social and political order" [14]. The deliberate lack of particularity in the two lovers, the fact that Julie, "the emblem of love, is par excellence the object that does not exist" [15], the extent of the substitution between Julie and her friend Claire d'Orbe; all are restructured by the apparent shift in perspective which is itself eventually destabilised by Julie's last letter, in which she attests that she had actually deluded herself (and of course us), in believing herself "cured" of love for St Preux (Letter XII, Part VI, p.405). The veil can now be seen to have meant also the veil of illusion over Julie's presumed innerness, her secret devotion to her lover that can only be confessed, like Dimmesdale's, in death.

Hawthorne's **Blithedale** does not propose such a severe undoing of the idea of love but it does establish a similar concern which is by no means allayed by Coverdale's ingenuous confession at the
80

end of his tale. The Veiled Lady, absent presence and focus of male desires in the novel, is a premonition of catastrophe. Discussing the implications of her performance the pale man in blue spectacles instances

> ...the miraculous power of one human being over the will and passions of another; insomuch that settled grief was but a shadow, beneath the influence of a man possessing this potency, and the strong love of years melted away like a vapor. At the bidding of one of these wizards the maiden, with her lover's kiss still burning on her lips, would turn from him with icy indifference; the newly made widow would dig up her buried heart out of her young husband's grave before the sods had taken root upon it; a mother; with her babe's milk in her bosom, would thrust away her child. Human character was but soft wax in his hands; and guilt, or virtue, only the forms into which he should see fit to mould it. The religious sentiment was a flame which he could blow up with his breath, or a spark that he could utterly extinguish" (III,198).

The origin of these instances of female treachery or indifference is Westervelt, whose patriarchal viciousness and cynical manipulation of the values of others suggests a further line of comparison with Rousseau's novel.

In both books we find a good father (Hollingsworth and Wolmar), and a bad father (Westervelt and Baron d'Etage, Julie's parent). Julie and St Preux are cast more or less as siblings, producing an incestuous atmosphere in their love affair [16]. This is also apparent in the relationship between Coverdale and Priscilla. In Coverdale's dream, he sees Hollingsworth and Zenobia bending over his bed like parents to exchange a kiss of sexual passion, while Priscilla, beholding the scene while peeping in at the window, "melted gradually away, and left only the sadness of her expression (III,153). Presumably her sadness of expression has to do with incompatibility between her love and sexual, perhaps parental, love, as Coverdale imagines this conflict. In La Nouvelle Heloise, Wolmar, the much older man who becomes Julie's undemonstrative husband, is of a cold nature, like Gervayse Hastings in Hawthorne's "The Christmas Banquet" (1846). Wolmar describes himself as having "a naturally tranquil mind and a cold heart. I am one of those men," he says, whom people think they are truly insulting when they call them insensible, that is, when they say they have no passion which diverts them from following the true direction of mankind. Little susceptible of pleasure and grief, I even experience only very faintly that sentiment of self-interest and humanitarianism which makes the affections of others our own. If I feel pain in seeing good people suffer, pity has no part in it, for I feel none in seeing the wicked suffer.... If I have any ruling passion it is that of observation" (Letter XII, Part IV, p.317). Wolmar combines Coverdale's detachment with Hollingsworth's tyranny, for his scheme of exorcising the love between St Preux and Julie _is_ a tyranny, however well based, like Hollingsworth's schemes, on high principles.

The fantasy family of **The Blithedale Romance** is much illuminated by comparison with Rousseau's **Nouvelle Heloise** because the latter novel draws attention to a facet of **Blithedale** which has been neglected in Freudian criticism's concern to see Coverdale as "a casualty of Oedipal strife" [17]. Instead of looking only at Coverdale's transference of sexual attraction from Zenobia to Priscilla we should also consider the relations between fantasy fathers and daughters. In **La Nouvelle Heloise** Julie's father holds a position of extraordinary and arbitrary power. Tony Tanner has described him as "the source of all those separations and divisions that ultimately derive from the prohibition of an incestuous return to undifferentiated oneness with the mother.... Julie's dream of total union [in the menage a trois at Clarens] is a projection into the future of a totally regressive urge. What she has to learn, though she resists it in every way she can, is that the world is a place of separations and divisions" [18]. In the episode in which she is violently assaulted by her father it is the lover who is reproached for his violation of the "otherwise blissful relationship" between the father and the daughter. With the mother approving their subsequent caresses, Tanner says,"this truly does offer a spectacle or scene that is pervaded by latent - and not so latent - incestuous feelings ... barely controlled incest" [19]. Julie writes, "I should think myself only too happy to be beaten every day for this reward, and there was no treatment so harsh that a single caress from him could not efface from my heart" (Letter LXIII, Part I, p.144). At the order of this patriarch Julie agrees to marry his old friend Wolmar and efface St Preux from her heart, along with the trace of her father's violence.

The incestuous situation in **Blithedale** is more overt, perhaps because the familial interrelations are rather suggested than literal. The fantasy family is composed of Zenobia as mother, Hollingsworth as father, Coverdale as son and Priscilla as daughter. Hollingsworth's turning away from Zenobia and his union with Priscilla is therefore scandalous to Coverdale and Zenobia because they perceive it as unnatural. This is the horror so well expressed by the frozen gesture of Zenobia's corpse and the sadistic damage to her breast inflicted by the boathook as Hollingsworth searches for her body. Zenobia's wealth passes on to the "daughter" who is more sexually attractive because she is hidden (forbidden, veiled); the "father", initially represented by Coverdale to be a paragon is then rejected for his incestuous fixation (and rivalry) and is finally presented as blasted by it, his potency cancelled by contact with its own narcissistic sources. To fulfil the tabooed desire is to short circuit supplementarity and abandon the substitutions such as reform schemes which drew energy from it [20]. The same message is conveyed in the transformation of Zenobia's flower into a jewelled imitation. In a gesture of savage irony, she hands this on through Coverdale to Priscilla.

But Coverdale occupies another "place" in the novel: as well as participating as a character he exists outside of his personal psychology. Coverdale's resemblance to his author has frequently struck commentators, as has his situation as artist: a minor poet anthologised by Griswold [21]. Attention to the "fourth side" locates Coverdale as the writer of the story, responsible for the narration, even to some extent the invention, of the events at Blithedale. **The Blithedale Romance** is Hawthorne's only major venture into fully characterised first person narration: his other novels and most of the tales employ an authorial narrator who is (with significant limitations in **The Marble Faun** and parts of **The Scarlet Letter**, omniscient). The result in **The Blithedale Romance** is a rather unformed novel in which the apparent clarity of the narrative technique is clouded by the uncertainties of the substance. Is Hollingsworth merely a calculating madman in adopting Priscilla after Zenobia loses her inheritance; and why should Coverdale miss the vital scene at Eliot's pulpit after having been almost magically present at the interview between Zenobia and Westervelt, or coincidentally just across the garden from her boarding house in town? The questions multiply and can only be resolved by postulating Coverdale as embodying the writing process itself, a creative alter ego standing in for the absent author. If read in this way the deeper logic behind Coverdale's dreams, which seem otherwise to be at odds with the ostensible realism of the narrative, becomes apparent.

In his first night at Blithedale Coverdale is feverish and suject to the torment of a fixed idea which, like the "nail in Sisera's brain" remains while "innumerable other ideas go and come, flutter to and fro, combining constant transition with intolerable sameness." This is an anticipation of what becomes his obsession with the three friends, against the background of reformers plans and projects. "Had I made a record of that night's half waking dreams," he continues, "it is my belief that it would have anticipated several of the chief incidents of the narrative, including a dim shadow of its catastrophe" (III,38). Coverdale is in the position of a writer who has conceived his plot's chief incidents, and its catastrophe, but sees them only as dim shadows, prior to their elaboration. The change in Arcadia to be experienced because of Zenobia's death is projected onto the fictional landscape expressionistically, along with an anticipation of the manner of her death: "I saw that the storm was past, and the moon was shining on the snowy landscape, which looked like a lifeless copy of the world in marble. From the bank of the distant river, which was shimmering in the moonlight, came the black shadow of the only cloud in heaven..." (III,38). Similar materials with a bearing on "the secret which was hidden even from themselves" (III,160), or expository of the "hieroglyphic" presented by Zenobia (III,162), appear in other dreams of Coverdale, both in his lodging house and when he falls asleep under the Pulpit Stone. Driven by his premonitions after this latter dream, Coverdale returns to a spot on the river where he had paused that afternoon, before encountering his friends. "I trod along by the dark, sluggish river, and remember pausing on the bank, above one of its blackest and most placid pools - (the very spot, with the barkless stump of a tree aslantwise over the water, is depicting itself to my fancy at this instant) - and wondering how deep it was, and if any overladen soul had ever flung its burden of mortality in thither, and if it ever escaped the burden, or only made it heavier" (III,207,208). In the course of this premonitory description we are being reminded of Coverdale the writer ("the very spot...is depicting itself to my fancy, at this instant"), and of the extent to which this text is modalised by its situation in time, supposedly being written twelve years after the events were supposed to have taken place. The displacements of time and Coverdale's memory of events years earlier put him in the position of a chronicler free to reimagine, even to reinvent his own history.

Accordingly, in a movement familiar in Hawthorne's work [22], the conversation Coverdale manages to overhear from his grape arbour is questioned as it is recounted. "Other mysterious words, besides what are above written, they spoke together; but I understood no more, and indeed even question whether I fairly understood so much as this. By long brooding over our recollections, we subtilize them into something akin to imaginary stuff, and hardly capable of being distinguished from it. In a few moments, they were completely beyond earshot"(III,104,105). This episode is an overt acknowledgement of what is everywhere covertly the case: the story is Coverdale's and its events are responsive to his imaginative presence as writer. In a moment of delirium he whispers to Hollinsgworth, "Zenobia is an enchantress! She is the sister of the Veiled Lady! That flower in her hair is a talisman. If you were to snatch it away, she would be transformed into something else!" (III,45). Or, thinking in terms of power to act presciently as well as to understand, Coverdale broods over his own reponsibility to his characters: "The thought impresses itself upon me, that I had left duties unperformed. With the power, perhaps, to act in the place of destiny, and avert misfortune from my friends, I had resigned them to their fate." But, he continues, "It now impresses me that, if I erred at all, in regard to Hollingsworth, Zenobia, and Priscilla, it was through too much sympathy, rather than too little" (III,154). The grounds of this assessment are lost in the penumbra of the novel he might have written,

or obscurely encoded in this one. Perhaps it is
Coverdale's excessive sympathy that propels the
three to their catastrophe: their sense of having
an audience that makes them perform, and thus
fulfill his needs rather than their own. This is
necessarily true of fiction, rather than history,
and a source of the guilt that Hawthorne
experienced as a writer.

In **The Blithedale Romance** Coverdale is put not
only in the place of the writer; he is also placed
as the reader, or audience. In the scene from which
the comments above were quoted, Coverdale, spying
from the window of his hotel on the new residents
of an opposite boarding house, finds himself in the
position of the helpless yet participating
spectator in whom the text has taken up its
existence: who is, therefore, doomed to a passive
act of creation [23].

> Nevertheless, there seemed something fatal in
> the coincidence that had borne me to this
> spot, of all others in a great city, and
> compelled me again to waste my already wearied
> sympathies on affairs which were none of mine,
> and persons who cared little for me. It
> irritated my nerves; it affected me with a
> kind of heart sickness. After the effort which
> it cost me to fling them off - after
> consummating my escape, as I thought, from
> these goblins of flesh and blood, and pausing
> to revive myself with a breath or two of an
> atmosphere in which they should have no share
> - it was a positive despair, to find the same
> figures arraying themselves before me, and
> presenting their old problem in a shape that
> made it more insoluble than ever.
> I began to long for a catastrophe. If the
> noble temper of Hollingsworth's soul were
> doomed to be utterly corrupted by the too
> powerful purpose, which had grown out of what
> was noblest in him; if the rich and generous
> qualities of Zenobia's womanhood might not
> save her; if Priscilla must perish by her
> tenderness and faith, so simple and so devout;
> -then be it so! Let it all come. As for me, I
> would look on, as it seemed my part to do,
> understandingly, if my intellect could fathom
> the meaning and the moral, and, at all events,
> reverently and sadly. The curtain fallen, I
> would pass onward with my poor individual
> life, which was now attenuated of much of its

proper substance, and diffused among many alien interests (III,157).

Coverdale presents his ennui as that of a spectator at a play, his "mental stage" on which the knot of characters are kept by "a real intricacy of events, greatly assisted by my method of insulating them from all other relations" (III,156). The theatrical metaphor is in keeping with the physical situation in the hotel's view of the opposite drawing room; yet it also holds the mirror up to the reader to show a further complicity of voyeurism. On other occasions the place of the reader is more fully defined: Coverdale likes to cast himself as the ideal spectator who has "that quality of the intellect and heart which impelled me, often against my own will, and to the detriment of my own comfort, to live in other lives, and to endeavour -by generous sympathies, by delicate intuitions, by taking note of things too slight for record, and by bringing my human spirit into manifold accordance with the companions whom God assigned me- to learn the secret which was hidden even from themselves" (III,160). His judgement might be "stern as that of Destiny itself" but would miss "no trait of original nobility of character, no struggle against temptation; no iron necessity of will, on the one hand, nor extenuating circumstance to be derived from passion and despair, on the other...." Nothing would go unappreciated, and although he might give "full assent to the punishment which was sure to follow," still it would be given mournfully, and "with undiminished love" (III,161). The perfect reader or spectator, of course, is very far from being the perfect friend: after this hymn to himself, and the invocation of a Shakesperian finale ("And, after all was finished, I would come, as if to gather up the white ashes of those who had perished at the stake, and to tell the world -the wrong being now atoned for - how much had perished there, which it had never yet known how to praise"), the self ironising Coverdale begins his next paragraph, "I sat in my rocking chair, too far withdrawn from the window to expose myself to another rebuke, like that already inflicted" (III,161). Coverdale's criticism of himself is implicitly a criticism of the reader, likewise seated safely away from the action which he wishes to enjoy and judge without cost. Zenobia implicitly indicts the reader as well as Coverdale when she says: "This long while past, you have been following up your game, groping for human emotions in the dark corners of the heart" (III,214).

But the narrative refuses him (and us) the satisfaction of complete knowledge, as if to evade the damnation of a final supplementarity or ultimate closure; something must be left unspecified. In the crucial scene missed by Coverdale he would have learned: "Zenobia's true character and history; the true nature of her mysterious connection with Westervelt; her later purpose towards Hollingsworth, and, reciprocally, his in reference to her; and, finally, the degree in which Zenobia had been cognisant of the plot against Priscilla, and what, at last, had been the real object of that scheme" (III,215). Hardened readers might be forgiven for wondering what else it might be the novel's business to tell us, if not this, and feeling that the author's unwillingness to answer these crucial questions is a failing comparable to the equivocations regarding Faun's ears in **The Marble Faun**. It may be, however, that these evasions register the degree of authorial perturbation over certain sorts of experience.

Coverdale's spectatorial presence, and the narrative's enunciation of questions that it does not intend to answer, foreground the issue of performance in **The Blithedale Romance**. To some extent the participants in the speculative community are play actors engaged in a pastoral masque, consciously in disguise and enjoying a consequent liberation from their society's constrictions. This is particularly evident in the Comus scene, when the reformers are actually in formal fancy dress (as opposed to the fancy dress they wear every day, while they enact the rituals of bucolic existence in suitable smocks). But within the charade there exist different levels of intensity; some characters seem to outperform others. Zenobia, for example, on her first appearance in the community, has the effect of causing the "heroic enterprise to show like an illusion, a masquerade, a pastoral, a counterfeit Arcadia, in which we grown-up men and women were making a play-day of the years that were given us to live in" (III,21). Coverdale attempts to analyse the causes of this impression, without success. Perhaps this failure is because one of the causes of his impression is Zenobia's adult sexuality, which demotes him to the status of child. Another reason for the effect created by Zenobia however must be her great suggestiveness. Her gestures are

88

creative like those of an actress: her "free, careless, generous modes of expression" often have an effect of creating images (III,17). A good example of her melodramatic expressiveness occurs when she first realises the threat posed by Priscilla: "Zenobia bade Hollingsworth good night very sweetly, and nodded to me with a smile. But just as she turned aside with Priscilla into the dimness of the porch, I caught another glance at her countenance. It would have made the fortune of a tragic actress, could she have borrowed it for the moment when she fumbles in her bosom for the concealed dagger, or the exceedingly sharp bodkin, or mingles the ratsbane in her lover's bowl of wine, or her rival's cup of tea" (III,78). Here, in fact, the acting consists not in the imitation of powerful feelings, but in the dissimulation involved in their denial. The melodramatic expression is actually the real one, which makes Coverdale's description doubly ironic: he is only able to conceive of emotion in terms of theatricality, just as as Zenobia is only able to act in the language of the theatre, whether she is on stage or off. But to notice this aspect of the novel is to notice in turn the theatrical aspect of the Brook Farm experiment in reviving Eden in West Roxbury, Massachusetts, in the eighteen forties.

NOTES

1. Jacques Derrida, "The Purveyer of Truth," **Yale French Studies** 52 (1975) pp.31-113. Lacan's "Seminar" on the Purloined Letter appeared in **Yale French Studies** 48 (1972).

2. Derrida "Purveyer," pp.78,79 and fn, p.79.

3. All references in the text are to **The Centenary Edition of the Works of Nathaniel Hawthorne** (Columbus: Ohio State University Press, 1964), vol III.

4. On the "supplement" see Derrida, **Of Grammatology**, (Baltimore & London: Johns Hopkins University Press,1974) pp.141-164. This quotation, p.147.

5. The arbitrariness of the sign in relation to any presumed "reality" is discussed in, for example, Terence Hawkes, **Structuralism and Semiotics** (London: Methuen, 1977) p.28.

6. Critical attacks on Coverdale's supposed inadequacies have been frequent. See Edgar Dryden,

Nathaniel Hawthorne: The Poetics of Enchantment (Ithaca: Cornell University Press, 1977), pp. 105, 106; or Rudolph Von Abele, The Death of the Artist (The Hague: Nijhoff, 1955) pp.74,76,81.

7. On negativity see, for example, Wolfgang Iser, The Implied Reader 1972 (Baltimore: Johns Hopkins University Press, 1974) p.46.

8. The critical preference for Zenobia has been general. See for example Nina Baym, The Shape of Hawthorne's Career (London: Cornell University Press, 1976) p.197.

9. Barthe's description is in La Plaisir du Texte tr. R. Miller (London: Jonathan Cape, 1976) p.9. Notice how the supplement operates here: "in Eve's earliest garment, i.e, naked, without a garment. Only the possibility of clothing can eroticise nudity. Compare "Counterfeit Art," herein.

10. John T. Irwin American Hieroglyphics (Newhaven & London: Yale University Press, 1980) pp.244, 267-269.

11. Irwin, p. 267.

12. Julie, or La Nouvelle Heloise tr. Judith H. McDowell (London: Pennsylvania State University Press, 1968).

13. The French and Italian Notebooks, The Centenary Edition, (Columbus: Ohio State University Press, 1980) vol XIV, pp.555-6.

14. Paul de Man, Allegories of Reading (New Haven and London: Yale University Press, 1979).

15. Paul de Man, p.216.

16. Paul de Man, 213.

17. Crews, The Sins of the Fathers p. 204. See also pp.194-212.

18. Tony Tanner, Adultery in the Novel (Baltimore and London: Johns Hopkins University Press, 1979) p.129.

19. Tanner, p.126.

20. This theme is further explored in "Counterfeit Nature" below.

21. Criticism on this aspect of Coverdale includes James Justus, "Hawthorne's Coverdale: Character and Art in The Blithedale Romance." American Literature 47 (1975) pp. 21-36.

22. Compare the discussion of an overheard conversation in The Marble Faun ("Counterfeit Nature," below).

23. See Georges Poulet, "Phenomenology of Reading," in New Literary History I (1969-70) pp.53-68.

The stress on acting in **The Blithedale Romance**
seems to have been both an expression of
Hawthorne's sense of the evasions involved in the
Blithedale / Brook Farm performance and a way for
him to avoid some of the autobiographical
responsibilities that weighed upon him in producing
a fictionalised account of his West Roxbury life.
The Preface demonstrates how this personal
necessity could be integrated with the artistic
dicta Hawthorne had earlier worked out: "In short,
his present concern with the Socialist Community is
merely to establish a theatre, a little removed
from the highway of ordinary travel, where the
creatures of his brain may play their
phantasmagorical antics, without exposing them to
too close a comparison with the actual events of
real life" (III,i). The desire to produce an
exemplary theatre, a little removed from
competition with "real life" also underlay the
reformers' intentions in the Roxbury experiment.
Quite how much of a show the Brook Farm community
could be is indicated by the number of visitors it
attracted, apparently as many as 4,000 a year [1],
and by the financial failure of Ripley's plan,
which had to be bailed out by eminent sympathisers.
Hawthorne, who became a trustee and one of the
three directors of the Association in September
1841, knew this aspect of the farm well, since his
own money was lost in the venture [2]. The
hypothesis of exemplary reform, that is, the
winning over of the larger society to a better form
of organisation through the success of example, was
one shared by many of the communist and socialist
societies in the American nineteenth century [3];
91

the idea had deep roots in American traditions, since this was the underlying premise of the Puritan settlers of New England: to build a city on a hill which would, by example alone, show the true way in religion to the world. The Blithedalers, aware of this parallel, often saw themselves as "descendants of the Pilgrims, whose high enterprise ... we had taken up, and were carrying it onward and aloft, to a point which they never dreamed of attaining" (III,117). The exemplary element, of course, cuts both ways: if the Blithedale community (and, by inference, Brook Farm), set an example to the rest of the world, their failure as much as their success might be exemplary: an indictment of the American experience, and a suggestion of reasons behind the larger failure.

Interpretations of **The Blithedale Romance** have frequently hinged upon the proposition that the community fails because its principles are against human nature, along the lines of Hollingsworth's criticism that, "There is not human nature in it!" (III,132) The romance, says Nina Baym, "does not pursue the socialist dimension of the experiment, restricting itself to the drama of the inner life"[4]. But it is a particular perversity that causes the catastrophe at Blithedale, not some supposedly universal passions of human nature. A perverse deadness is at the centre of the disastrous vortex, a deadness that absorbs the life and passions of others into itself:

> Nature thrusts some of us into the world miserably incomplete, on the emotional side, with hardly any sensibilities except what pertain to us as animals. No passion, save of the senses; no holy tenderness, nor the delicacy that results from this. Externally, perhaps, they bear a close resemblance to other men, and have perhaps all save the finest grace; but when a woman wrecks herself on such a being, she ultimately finds that the real womanhood within her has no corresponding part in him. Her deepest voice lacks a response; the deeper her cry, the more dead his silence (III,103).

This description (of Westervelt, in fact, not Hollingsworth), echoes throughout the novel. Michael Davitt Bell identifies the failure of Blithedale's community as a failure to "confront the full implications of the imaginative regeneration they claim to espouse," which thus turns the "veil of symbolic expression into a mask of evasion," a masquerade [5]. The Blithedalers have espoused "ideality," a sentimentalised evasion of their own ideals which, in its ultimate manifestations, has the deadness of the spirit world called up by Westervelt's mesmerism. "The account of Westervelt's spiritualism reveals how fully ... even the antiformal impulse of spiritual regeneration has become a species of formal, mechanical artifice" [6]. And Priscilla, whose "impalpable grace lay so singularly between disease and beauty" (III,101), is in these respects a premonition of the fate of all, notwithstanding her privileged position as focus of desire within the text. She is the hidden implication of Westervelt's "idealism," resident spirit of Summerland at Blithedale.

It is possible also to see Blithedale as part of another, artistic, failure: the failure of American Romanticism in its refusal to acknowledge the "reality of social and psychological disrelation" [7]. The corollary of this view, however, is that Zenobia be presented as fulfilling the Romantic possibility: "Of the utopians we meet, only Zenobia comes anywhere near to trusting the community's alleged 'spirit'" [8]. Bell is not the only critic to portray a romantic Hawthorne, whose criticism of the Blithedale society is that it does not fulfill its own radical premise. Nina Baym would agree:

> The dangers it exposes are of the repressive and punishing forces that will permanently damage the personality if given the opportunity. Such dangers threaten not only the individual personality but society as a whole. Hollingsworth finally becomes his own victim; his repudiation of Zenobia is suicidal. There are no people without passion, and no societies without people. To extinguish passion is to extinguish life. In the civilised man, passion is already more than adequately controlled. It is control itself that needs boundaries [9].

But it is precisely that romantic vision of a possible integration of the self and other, self and society (which William James called "healthy mindedness" [10]), to be achieved through recognising the passional self, and throwing off

93

societal restraints, that Hawthorne is so carefully
unpicking. To abandon Zenobia and embrace Priscilla
is certainly a fatal choice of daughter over
mother, tabooed object over totem object, the
signifier over the signified. But it is not
representative of surplus control. On the contrary,
it pursues the erotic to the point of breakdown,
anticipating Huysmans and Baudelaire and evoking de
Sade. What Hawthorne manages to do, by analysing
the outer life of Blithedale through its inner
travails, is to investigate the "bats and owls, and
the host of night-birds, which flapped their dusky
wings against the gazer's eyes, and sometimes were
mistaken for birds of angelic feather" in the
circles of reform (X,31). Nor does Zenobia escape
this fowler's net: she is only the greatest actress
among them all, a "tragedy queen" whose hard won
feminist opinions collapse at a word from
Hollingsworth (III,123,124), and whose deepest
emotions surface in the cliches of melodrama:

> And so you kiss this poor, despised, rejected
> hand! Well, my dear friend, I thank you! You
> have reserved your homage for the fallen. Lip
> of man will never touch my hand again. I
> intend to become a Catholic, for the sake of
> going into a nunnery. When you next hear of
> Zenobia, her face will be behind the black
> veil; so look your last at it now - for all is
> over! Once more, farewell! (III,227,228)

Coverdale's comment on her death is that there was
in it "some tint of the Arcadian affectation" that
had been visible in the lives of the Blithedalers,
and he regrets that the world "has come to an
awfully sophisticated pass, when ... we cannot even
put ourselves to death in whole-hearted simplicity"
(III,237).

Whatever the community's failure to
acknowledge the "dark night of the soul, confronted
by their great European and British contemporaries"
[11], that failure is not Hawthorne's. He pursues
the problem of disrelation to its roots, not in the
affectations of dark romanticism (which simply
express the other side of inspiration, [12]), but
in the perverse deadness of behaviour which
afflicts even Zenobia. The only truth in her life
or death is the damage inflicted to her body by
Hollingsworth's boathook, and that is not "true" in
the moralised version of the narrative ("You have
wounded the poor thing's breast ... close by her

heart, too!" III,235) but rather as an expression
of the covert sexual sadism which runs throughout
the novel and is modelled in the relationship
between Priscilla and Westervelt.

The petrification of desire in supplementarity
requires that any vitality there is be expressed
violently, as in sadistic sexuality. This
recognition is secretly made in Hawthorne's other
novels, especially **The Scarlet Letter** and **The
Marble Faun**. But in **The Blithedale Romance** it is
forced to the surface, in response to the degree to
which the novel analyses the conditions of everyday
life and admits some of the difficulties that were
glossed over in the new sexuality of **The House of
the Seven Gables**. Blithedale takes its place
alongside Fitzgerald's **The Great Gatsby** and West's
The Day of the Locust in coming to such conclusions
regarding the promise of American life and
expressing them in images of sexual mutilation as
the fullest embodiment of displaced desires [13].
Blithedale thus casts a ghastly light back over
several of Hawthorne's tales, notably "Rappaccini's
Daughter" (discussed in Chapter One) and "The
Birthmark" (March 1843) which demonstrates close
affinities with Hawthorne's meditations on
"reform."

Coverdale, and perhaps also the reader, is
surprised by Zenobia's collaboration with her ugly
fate when, confronted with Hollingsworth's disdain,
which degrades women to the role of mere
accessories to men, her feminism crumbles and she
subsequently chooses the death of a betrayed
village maiden, leaving Coverdale for once in
agreement with Westervelt: "It was an idle thing -
a foolish thing - for Zenobia to do .... She had
life's summer all before her, and a hundred
varieties of brilliant success!" (III,239)
Westervelt offers a cynical, more "scientific,"
view of sexuality: "Her heart! ... that troublesome
organ (as she had hitherto found it) would have
been kept in its due place and degree, and have had
all the gratification it could fairly claim. She
would soon have established a control over it"
(III,240). This provokes an indignant response from
Coverdale, which is to some extent misleading.
Coverdale's is the narrative voice, but
Westervelt's might be called the voice of the text:
skeptical about "love," probing the origins of
desire and observing its perversions, and the
necessity of those perversions given the role of
signification in desire. Nor is this simply the

voice of the author, that "Hawthorne" we infer from
the text, it is the voice of the age, offering new
forms of discourse about sexuality [14].

Michel Foucault argues that, far from being
the age of repression in which sexuality was no
longer a legitimate subject of discourse, the
nineteenth century and our own "have been rather
the age of multiplication: a dispersion of
sexualities, a strengthening of their disparate
forms, a multiple implantation of 'perversions'"
[15]. Medicine especially entered the area of
sexuality where "it created an entire organic,
functional, or mental pathology arising out of
'incomplete' sexual practises; it carefully
classified all forms of related pleasure; it
incorporated them into notions of 'development' and
instinctual 'disturbances'; and it undertook to
manage them" [16]. Foucault sees this "forceful
entry into the pleasures of the couple" not in
terms of the level of indulgence or repression
involved but in terms of the form of power that was
thereby exercised: "Power operated as a mechanism
of attraction; it drew out those peculiarities over
which it kept watch. Pleasure spread to the power
that harried it; power anchored the pleasure it
uncovered" [17]. Westervelt, like Chillingworth, or
like Aylmer in "The Birthmark", has such a
relationship to the facts of love and sexuality.
Nor should we fail to observe the complicity of
other interested parties: Hester, who keeps
Chillingworth's secret; Dimmesdale, who conspires
in the process of his own victimising; Zenobia, who
has been married to Westervelt and still colludes
with him; Priscilla, who accepts his domination; or
Georgiana, who encourages Aylmer's fatal scientific
idealism; and Beatrice Rappaccini, who swallows the
draught she knows will destroy her, the antidote to
life. As an observer of the mores of his period,
Hawthorne participated in this new recognition of
sexualities, as did Melville, or Flaubert.
Foucault's description of the development of
"perversions" seems particularly apposite to such
writers: "These polymorphous conducts were actually
extracted from people's bodies and from their
pleasures; or rather, they were solidified in them;
they were drawn out, revealed isolated,
intensified, incorporated by multifarious power
devices. The growth of perversion is not a
moralising theme that obsessed the scrupulous minds
of the Victorians. It is the real product of the
encroachment of a type of power on bodies and their
96

pleasures. [The West] has defined new rules for the
game of powers and pleasures. The frozen
countenance of the perversions is a fixture of this
game" [18]. There could hardly be a better
description of the activities of Hawthorne's
knowers and their victims or, to turn the screw
again, of "Hawthorne."

"The Birthmark," written in March 1843, not
long after Hawthorne's personal experience of
"reform" in the relations between the sexes at
Brook Farm in 1841, and soon after his marriage,
during the period of "Eden" at the Old Manse,
offers an example of what the medical profession
would soon be in a position to call the
sado-masochistic perversion. Georgiana's small red
mark, shaped (significantly) like a hand, which
comes and goes with the flush of blood in her
cheek, is taken by Aylmer, then by herself, and
ultimately by the text too, as an emblem of the
earthly imperfection in her beauty. The "bloody
hand" shocks and obsesses Aylmer, until his reading
of it causes him more trouble and horror than her
beauty had given him delight (X,39). After
Georgiana conspires with him to have the hand
removed, saying that "life, while this hateful mark
makes me the object of your horror and disgust -
life is a burden which I would fling down with joy.
Either remove this dreadful Hand or take my
wretched life!" Aylmer comes closer to
acknowledging his deeper desires: "Do not shrink
from me! Believe me, Georgiana, I even rejoice in
this single imperfection, since it will be such
rapture to remove it" (X,44).

The repeated stress on the entanglement of the
hand with the deepest sources of the woman's life:
"The fatal Hand had grappled with the mystery of
life, and was the bond by which an angelic spirit
kept itself in union with a mortal frame" (X,55);
or, "it may be the stain goes as deep as life
itself ... the firm gripe of this little hand which
was laid upon me before I came into the world"
(X,41); seems to provide for a complete
recuperation of the story as a male response to
female sexuality [19], or, more exactly, to
menstruation, as is indicated by the numerous
references to blood associated with the hand.
Aylmer even dreams of the operation in which,
assisted by the gross Aminadab, he attempts to
remove the hand but "the deeper went the knife, the
deeper sank the Hand, until at length its tiny
grasp appeared to have caught hold of Georgiana's

heart; whence, however, her husband was inexorably
resolved to cut or wrench it away" (X,40). The
actual operation, by necromantic cordial (like
Beatrice's), is accompanied by Aylmer's "almost
irrepressible ecstasy" (X,55). These aspects make
it possible for critics to read the tale
confidently towards their own moral: not
Hawthorne's "he failed to look beyond the shadowy
scope of Time, and, living once for all in
Eternity, to find the perfect Future in the
present" (X,56) [which is indeed, contradictory
enough to give one pause]; but, in Crews' version,
"the libido sciendi, in a word, appears to have a
good deal of libido in it" ... the story is "a
fantasy of sadistic revenge and a scarcely less
obvious sexual consummation" [20].

     This does not delve deeply enough: Aylmer and
Georgiana both prefer the supplement to the sexual
consummation for which the critics propose it
stands. "She felt how much more precious was such a
sentiment than that meaner kind which would have
borne with the imperfection for her sake, and have
been guilty of treason to holy love by degrading
its perfect idea to the level of the actual"
(X,52). The crystal goblet satisfies her as well as
Aylmer: "it allays a feverish thirst that had
parched me for many days," and it gives her a
narcissistically pleasurable sensation: "My earthly
senses are closing over my spirit like the leaves
around the heart of a rose at sunset" (X,54). The
improvement offered by the story, although
officially contradicted by the narrator, is the
discovery of a new form of sexuality which replaces
the old. The narrator's version, quoted above,
displays a startling evasiveness: "Living once for
all in Eternity," Aylmer should "find the perfect
Future in the Present"; perhaps in the same way
that Georgiana finds more beauty in the artificial
pictures that are screened for her than in the real
objects they represent: "The scenery and pictures
were perfectly represented, but with that
bewitching, yet indescribable difference which
always makes a picture, an image, or a shadow so
much more attractive than the original" (X,45).
That displacement makes "perversion" inevitable, as
soon as the alternative is preferred to the
"actual."

     The Hand itself requires attention; it appears
everywhere in the tale, like the letter in **The
Scarlet Letter**, sometimes in a very subdued
patterning which may be missed by casual reading:
98

"In his grasp, the veriest clod of earth assumed a soul" (X,49), conceals the motif, as does Aylmer's description of a poison: "By its aid I could apportion the lifetime of any mortal at whom you might point your finger" (X,47), or the apparently routine usage in the idea that the philosopher might ultimately "lay his hand on the secret of creative force" (X,36). Another conventional usage is of the hand as a marker of writing, as in "a large folio from her husband's own hand," as melancholy as ever "mortal hand had penned" (X,48,49), echoing "the spectral Hand that wrote mortality where he would fain have worshipped" (X,39). The identification of the hand with the pen returns us to the sinister question of the written: all Aylmer's great experiments reduce ultimately to the record of their failure in a folio, as this one will become the written story of "The Birthmark" [21]. The hand is itself a writing on Georgiana, its meaning of mortality conceals associated connotations including sexuality, the female body, reproduction, the sexual wound, or masturbation [22]. Aylmer cannot bear that his wife should be already inscribed; she, similarly, cannot bear that her own perfect body should be marred, outside of her own control, vulnerable to history, biology and the effects of time. "The crimson hand expressed the ineludible gripe in which mortality clutches the highest and purest of earthly mould, degrading them into kindred with the lowest, and even with the very brutes, like whom their visible frames return to dust" (X,39). Aylmer's aims resemble those of Frankenstein, but in another register: he has abandoned his researches into the creation of life; the monster already exists and she should be purified of all the constituting mortality. Frankenstein's monster was composed of bits and pieces of human anatomy stolen from graves; material which determines the monster's response to the rejection of his benevolent intentions. It is a form of the return of the repressed, the undead. To this extent, whatever additional issues of monstrous birth or abortion are covertly indicated, Mary Shelley propagandises life and the natural. But Hawthorne's story itemises the triumph of sadomasochism and artificiality in a crescendo against which the pasted-on moralism of the conclusion is unconvincing. Georgiana encourages Aylmer not to repent that "with so pure and high a feeling" he has "rejected the best that earth could offer" (X,55). She is dying, but that is her apotheosis, her deepest desire, for which she conspired with her lover. The story pretends to the conclusion: She is perfect, but alas, she is dead! It secretly concludes: She is dead but [therefore] she is perfect! This reminds of Poe in its perverse rejection of "the best that earth could offer," and even seems to quote extensively from "Ligeia" in its assemblage of trappings, the shifting draperies of Georgiana's chamber, the alchemical devices of Aylmer, the library of occult readings; it is, of course, contemporaneous with Poe's horror tale, but it is more exact in its elucidation of the origins of a turning against life, substituting a knowledge of obsession with the signifier for Poe's morbid confusion.

The reformed sexuality of "The Birthmark" led on to further investigations of desire in the following year, "The Artist of the Beautiful," Rappaccini's Daughter," and "Drowne's Wooden Image" were all written in 1844. The first two of these I have already discussed, and their relation to the "perverse" choice of the artificial over the natural should be apparent. "Drowne's Wooden Image" seems more inncocent at first, like "Feathertop," (1852) or "The Snow Image" (1850), it centres on the idea of the coming to life of an inanimate object, in a simple period fable. The woodcarver Drowne falls in love with a beautiful woman: his love causes his work to reach a higher realm of art in imitation, so that the unexpected presence of the woman walking through the streets seems to the townspeople to be Drowne's carved figurehead come to life. At a superior level of interpretation, it is Drowne himself who comes alive, ceasing to be as wooden as his own carved figures and striking the artist Copley as displaying genius in his art.

There is, however, a good deal of obscure sexual innuendo in this tale: if we pay attention to the names we find that the captain of the brig "Cynosure" for which this figurehead is carved is called Hunnewell [Honey well], which gives a strong sexual suggestion regarding the foreign lady's "piquancy of mirthful mischief" and "bewitching coquetry," or her "voluptuous mouth" and the flowers of Eden in her hat (X,314,316,317); and leads to another pun, on the woodcarver's name: he "drownes" in this honeypot. After his brief sexual awakening Drowne returns, wilfully it seems, to the "mechanical" style of his earlier productions, ending his days as a confirmed bachelor, Deacon Drowne. But Drowne has a symbolic revenge on

100

Arcadian Affectations

Captain Hunnewell, who put temptation in his way
only to remove it: a "reduced likeness of his
friend Captain Hunnewell, holding a telescope and
quadrant - may be seen to this day at the corner of
Broad and State Streets, serving in the useful
capacity of sign to the shop of a nautical
instrument maker" (X,319). Hunnewell is shrunken to
the place of a signifier, like another of Drowne's
images of lost potency, the Indian chief, gilded
all over, which stood for most of a century on the
cupola of the Province House, dazzling the eyes of
any who looked up at it, like an angel of the sun
(X,319).

Attached to this story is the moral "that the
very highest state to which a human spirit can
attain, in its loftiest aspirations, is its truest
and most natural state, and that Drowne was more
consistent with himself when he wrought the
admirable figure of the mysterious lady than when
he perpetrated a whole progeny of blockheads"
(X,320). Since it obscures the area of sexual
tension underlying Drowne's artistry, that moral
seems disingenuous, and is the more so in its
incorporation of the reproductive metaphor, as the
theme of "progeny" exists elsewhere in references
to Drowne's "worthless abortions" (X,311). The
creation of a completely lifelike simalcrum of a
woman is generally in Hawthorne's work a guilty
activity, as the strictures on nudity in art in **The
Marble Faun** indicate. Drowne's image is
conspicuously clothed, as if to forestall that
charge, but her dress (and that of her original) is
provocative, exotic, not quite decent; "fantastic,"
yet "not too fantastic to be worn decorously in the
street" (X,314), which has the effect of indicating
how near she does come to indecorum. South Seas
exotica, verging on the pornographic given the
period's suppressions, was a popular literary mode,
as Melville knew: is this not the reason for the
suggestiveness of this lady from the isle of Fayal,
a slightly lascivious Eden?

The duplicity of "morals"in Hawthorne's tales
deserves some consideration. As he noted in the
Preface to **The House of the Seven Gables**, the
establishing of a moral may seem to resemble the
transfixing pin by which a butterfly is mounted: it
transforms the original tale into a type, or a
member of a species, at the cost of any individual
life. There can be an embarrassment in one's
attendance at these performances which increases
the temptation to see Hawthorne's ostensible morals
101

as deceptive, subversive of his genteel culture's expectations. The moment of attachment of the moral is, of course, the moment of interaction between the imaginative work and the claims of the society in which it is produced. Only at this point are those claims admitted, rehearsed, or parodied and refused. Hawthorne's relation to his society was especially problematic: as the self-appointed recluse, silent even among friends, a mystery even to his wife, the confiding author, writing out of his depths to the unknown and possibly nonexistent sympathising reader; yet at the same time the public man, a politician at times, gaining high office in recognition of his services to the presidential campaign of Pierce, and holding posts as publicly visible and engaged as Customs Surveyer or American Consul at Liverpool. Admired and reviled as he then inevitably was, Hawthorne had reasons enough for deviousness in his admissions of the meaning of his writings. Another nexus adds further complications: the Peabody drawing room was a centre for transcendental reform; Sophia appears to have been an ardent believer in the new dispensation, and Hawthorne and she lived in Concord. A whole dimension of moral readings follow immediately from this, as Sophia and Hawthorne in effect collaborated on the proper meaning of a tale, its point of entry into the society.

The appended moral is a curious device inasmuch as the literary text is already composed of a series of instructions for the production of meaning, as Wolfgang Iser has shown: "The iconic signs of literature constitute an organization of signifiers which do not serve to designate a signified object, but instead designate instructions for the production of the signified" [24]. To offer further formal instructions suggests either that the embedded instructions that comprise the text may be ambiguous or that they may be heretical as regards the religious, ethical, economic or sexual taboos of the society within which it is produced. Or the appended moral may be expressive of the society's tendency to moralised readings of objects and events, and its fears of what may be uncovered by the free imagination. Both integration and alienation, then, are equally possible determinants of this practise. Hawthorne's provision of morals for his stories displays a movement towards and away from his society: there is a desire for formal accountability and a need to defuse some of the disturbing implications of the
102

fiction; there is equally a forestalling of the act of criticism, which in his period was predominantly moralistic [25], by its incorporation within the text. To moralise a story is to take possession of it: by incorporating the criticism within the text the author (and here Hawthorne resembles the post-modernist writer), may build in structures that incapacitate future criticism by subverting its positions. The author inserts the pin into the butterfly and names the species, but perhaps he deliberately misclassifies it. "Wakefield," (1835) will serve as an example of the technique. It "leaves us much food for thought, a portion of which shall lend its wisdom to a moral; and be shaped into a figure. Amid the seeming confusion of our mysterious world, individuals are so nicely adjusted to a system, and systems to one another, and to a whole, that, by stepping aside for a moment, a man exposes himself to a fearful risk of losing his place forever" (IX,140). As every reader notices, Wakefield's "moment" is an absence of twenty years, during which his wife has slowly settled into widowhood, never actually replacing her vanished husband. So Hawthorne's moral is far from establishing an unequivocal reading of the tale. But it does serve as an example of the peculiar form of transcendentalist moralising which so often wears a secondhand air in Hawthorne's fiction and notebook musings: as though earnest attempts are being made to see the world as transparently as through the eyes of Emerson or the Peabodys, but however stubbornly the sky is sought on the surface of a mud puddle it remains a reflection, and the "goldmine" is a dungheap after all. These morals may be read as counterparts to Hawthorne's subtly confusing prefaces, a combination which, through framing, offers the story some independence of being. When a moral is not expressly supplied we frequently find some equivalent statement, like Coverdale's admission of love for Priscilla, or the afterword in **The Marble Faun** and the enigmatic heraldic emblem at the end of **The Scarlet Letter**, which somewhat mystifies the straightforward advice to "be true!"

Attention to the moral as formal device returns us to the general question of staging: the relationship between the work and the audience given recognition by an address <u>outside</u> the text itself; the "fourth side." But just as in theatre the fourth side is <u>always</u> present, whether or not the stage manager stands before the curtains in

prologue or epilogue, so in Hawthorne's writing a
tendency towards moralised closure is always
apparent. The text contains its own commentary,
yet, like the appended moral, the commentary fails
quite to fit its circumstances. When the voice is
most magisterial, the discrepancy is most marked.
Hester, for example, has thought much about the
relations between the sexes, and speculated upon
the difficulties in the way of change. The narrator
comments that "a woman never overcomes these
problems by any exercise of thought. They are not
to be solved, or only in one way. If her heart
chance to come uppermost, they vanish" (I,166). As
a comment on Hester's situation, and implicitly
that of women generally, this is at odds with the
care taken to establish the contours of her actual
historical position and its intractability. The
more dangerous the material in respect of the
taboos and traumas of Hawthorne's culture, it
seems, the more noticeable are these moralised
interventions, as though the reader must not be
allowed simply to read but must be instructed how
to interpret what is read. Hawthorne, as he
instructs us that Beatrice Rappaccini really is a
heavenly angel, or that Hester has learned much
that is amiss, behaves as though he were at one and
the same time the showman (Westervelt, the German
Jew of "Ethan Brand" with his diorama, the
exhibitor of "Main Street,"the story teller of
"Alice Doane's Appeal"); and yet still the
judicious commentator, the magistrate, perhaps even
the authoritarian puritan who assesses the relative
merits of jollity and gloom. We must, then, take
seriously his desire to open an intercourse with
the world (IX,6), since that intercourse so
determines the textual surface, if not its deeper
structures. The struggle between the audience and
the play is continually a cause for concern,
constantly requiring mediation and sometimes, one
suspects, placation. It is frequently foregrounded
as the subject of a sketch or tale, as happens in
"Main Street" or "Alice Doane's Appeal," or it may
be enacted by a character within a story, as by
Coverdale, or Giovanni in "Rappaccini's Daughter."
Some of Hawthorne's sketches consist almost
entirely of this relationship, becoming lists, like
"A Select Party" or "The Hall of Fantasy," in which
the appeal lies only in the act of mediation: who
will the author include; how justly will he he
characterise each figure; and with what degree of
wit? That such productions should be popular
104

literary pieces says much about the contemporary exacerbation of author - audience relations. Hawthorne acknowledged the difficulty he felt in this area, as when he remarked "it is a very suspicious symptom of the deficiency of the popular element in a book, when it calls forth no harsh criticism" (IX,7). To be popular is to be the showman, and to be criticised [26]. An attempt may be made to defuse that criticism by its incorporation within the text, however, as Hawthorne attempts in his morals and commentary, or in prefatory remarks. In the preface to **Twice Told Tales** he criticises his work for its tepidity, and asks that it be read in the "clear, brown, twilight atmosphere in which it was written; if opened in the sunshine, it is apt to look exceedingly like a volume of blank pages" (IX,5). The productions of fancy require a sympathetic audience; or should we say that exposed to a critical scrutiny the reprehensible meanings will flee the page and leave it innocently blank? There seems to be a parallel between the writing that disappears and the writing that the author burns, as was Hawthorne's habit with his first drafts and early productions, a habit celebrated in "The Devil in Manuscript" (1835) a title revelatory of his sense of the artist - audience confrontation [27]. Perhaps there is a parallel between the writing that petrifies and is at last burned in "Earth's Holocaust" and the imaginative life which, paradoxically, only writing makes possible, an Edenic naturalness and innocence contradicted by the very act of knowing it and writing it down.

NOTES

1. Robert Cantwell, **Nathaniel Hawthorne: The American Years** (New York: Rinehart & Co, 1948) p.322, quoted from O.B. Frothingham's **George Ripley** (Boston: Houghton Mifflin, 1882).

2. Arlin Turner, **Nathaniel Hawthorne: A Biography** (New York: Oxford University Press, 1980), p.133. On September 28, 1841, Hawthorne became a trustee and one of the three directors of finance.

3.There is a valuable firsthand account of the various communities in Charles Nordhoff, **The Communistic Societies of the United States** (1875, New York: Hillary House, 1960). See also Alice

Felt Tyler, **Freedom's Ferment: Phases of American Social History** from the Colonial Period to the Outbreak of the Civil War (1944, New York: Harper & Row, 1962).
    4. Nina Baym, **The Shape of Hawthorne's Career** (Ithaca and London: Cornell University Press, 1976) p.189.
    5. Michael Davitt Bell, **The Development of American Romance: The Sacrifice of Relation** (Chicago: University of Chicago Press, 1980) p191.
    6. Bell, p.186.
    7. Bell, p.187.
    8. Bell, p.188.
    9. Baym, p.201.
    10. William James, **The Varieties of Religious Experience** (London: Collins Fountain, 1979) Lecture IV.
    11. Bell, p.187.
    12. See Robert Adams, **Nil: Episodes in the Literary Conquest of Void during the Nineteenth Century** (New York: Oxford University Press, 1966). See also Morse Peckham, "Towards a Theory of Romanticism" **PMLA** 66 (1951) pp. 5-23.
    13. This follows Larzer Ziff's view in **Literary Democracy** (New York: Viking Press, 1981), that sexual symbols may be symbolic of larger social concerns, which reverses the usual critical procedure whereby "objects and gestures presumably representing publicly admissible meanings can be seen to be sexual symbols." p.137. The parallel to **The Great Gatsby** in which Myrtle Wilson's breast is torn off is very striking.
    14. G. J. Barker-Benfield offers the essential documenting of these new views of sexual perversion in **The Horrors of the Half-Known Life: Male Attitudes to Women and Sexuality in Nineteenth Century America** (New York: Harper Colophon, 1977).
    15. Michel Foucault, **The History of Sexuality,** Vol One, tr. by Robert Hurley (Harmondsworth: Penguin Books, 1981) p. 37.
    16. Foucault, p.41.
    17. Foucault, p.45.
    18. Foucault, p.48.
    19. Frederick Crews, **The Sins of the Fathers** (New York: Oxford University Press, 1966) p. 126; Simon O. Lesser, **Fiction and the Unconscious** (Boston: Harvard University Press, 1957) pp.87-90.
    20. Crews,. p.126.
    21. See Jacques Derrida, "Freud and the Scene of Writing," in **Writing and Difference** tr. Alan Bass (London: Routledge and Kegan Paul, 1981)

pp.196-231.
22. The significance of the hand as sexual motif is explored in my chapter "Footprints in Sand," below. In Hawthorne's period it became a euphemism for masturbation, as in "Pouring out by the hand (the vicious act of Onan)," John Todd, quoted in Barker-Benfield, p.170. A strong connection was also made between reading and masturbation: ibid, p.167.
23. See T. Walter Herbert, **Marquesan Encounters: Melville and the Meaning of Civilization** (Cambridge: Harvard University Press, 1980) pp. 14,15.
24. Wolfgang Iser, "The Reality of Fiction: A Functionalist Approach to Literature," **New Literary History** 7 (1975-6), p.18.
25. Terence Martin, **The Instructed Vision** (Bloomington: Indaian University Press, 1961) discusses the relations between criticism and authors in this period.
26. This argument is somewhat along the lines of Rudolph Von Abele's **The Death of the Artist** (The Hague: Nijhoff, 1955), p. 50 and passim.
27. See also Jean Normand, **Nathaniel Hawthorne: An Approach to an Analysis of Artistic Creation** (Cleveland: Press of Case Western Reserve University, 1970) p.162.

COUNTERFEIT NATURE: THE MARBLE FAUN

In **The Marble Faun** Hawthorne's descriptions of the Borghese gardens, and of Donatello's response to them, are of peculiar interest in establishing how the concept of Nature is brought into question even as it is introduced. The gardens exemplify both terms of the title, the Marble and the Faun, in the artfulness with which they imitate a hypothetical "golden age" and develop the characterization of Donatello as representative of its inhabitants. The Faun, exemplar of naturalness, a missing link between man and the animals, has been discovered in the marble of Praxitele's statue at the opening of the novel: "Only a sculptor of the finest imagination could have succeeded in imprisoning the sportive and frisky thing, in marble" (IV,10) [1]. Donatello is the living version of the Faun, who will in the course of the story be himself immured physically in prison, and spiritually in guilt, and thereby become "human"; in the Gardens he is shown at first in his original state, modelling the simple and direct relationship to the natural that is implicit in the golden age myth, but the impossibility of such a relationship in the present, if ever, and least of all in Rome, is indicated by the numerous references to falseness, imitation, and death that the chapter contains.

A skepticism about the possibility of a golden age is evident in Hawthorne's **French and Italian Notebooks**, in an entry of June 16th, 1858: "This morning I went with Miss Shephard and Una to the Uffizzi gallery, and again looked with more or less attention at almost every picture and statue. I saw a little picture of the golden age, in which the charms of youths and virgins are depicted with a freedom that this iron age can hardly bear to look at" (XIV,321). The painting, by Jacopo Zucchi,c.1541-1589/90, in the Uffizzi Gallery, entitled "The Golden Age"[2], does indeed display an enthusiastic impropriety, including the embraces of lovers and the rivalry of children urinating, and showing grotesque figures on the mountain behind, one of whom seems to be inventing the alphabet. Hawthorne's response (or should we say the lack of it?) is striking, in the rapidity with which he addresses himself to contemporary exclusions, and avoids all the appeals of the originary myth. This "iron age" will have none of it, just as the "iron man" Endicott would have no revelling around maypoles in the New World.

Donatello's supposedly "leaf-shaped" and furry ears (IV,71) are as near as Hawthorne is prepared to come in enumerating the "charms" of his youth and virgin, and even these have to remain invisible (like the mere possibility of a "caudal appendage" which is hidden by the lion's skin in the Faun of Praxiteles) for this is an area in which Donatello is said to be excessively sensitive; it had "always been a tender point with my forefathers and me" (IV,12). So the possibility of scandal is noted, but immediately avoided, producing an area of reticence ("I entreat you to take the tips of my ears for granted" IV,12), one that Hawthorne felt impelled to take up in his Postscript, added to reduce, if only a little, the mysteries of which so many readers and reviewers had complained: "'Only one question more,' said I, with intense earnestness. 'Did Donatello's ears resemble those of the Faun of Praxiteles?' 'I know, but may not tell,' replied Kenyon, smiling mysteriously. 'On that point, at all events, there shall be not one word of explanation'" (IV,467). This concludes the novel. Hawthorne's idea that the conceit of faun's ears on a man might be lightly passed over was not the case, in practise, and he registered his imperfect success in having to make any further explanation at all: "The idea of the modern Faun, for example, loses all the poetry and beauty which the Author fancied in it, and becomes nothing better than a grotesque absurdity, if we bring it into the actual light of day" (IV,463); and, "The idea grows coarse, as we handle it, and hardens in our grasp" (IV,10). "He had hoped to mystify this anomalous creature between the Real and the Fantastic, in such a manner that the reader's

110

sympathies might be excited to a certain pleasurable degree, without impelling him to ask how Cuvier would have classified poor Donatello, or to insist upon being told, in so many words, whether he had furry ears or not. As respects all who ask such questions, the book is, to that extent, a failure" (IV,464). But surely the presumed furry ears are a signal not simply of the Faun's poetry and beauty, but of its outrageousness, as regards the decorum of the "iron age": they stand for all that is passed over in the censorious nineteenth century America; the golden age is dangerous, erotic, tolerable only for its ignorance, of which the grotesque correction lurks in the background, in the figure of the beginning of the alphabet; ABCDEFG: hence the embarassment of the "Author".

In the effort to render the scandalous faun more respectable several strategies are adopted. The aspect of satyr is displaced onto the demonic model, who "was clad in a voluminous cloak, that seemed to be made of a buffalo's hide, and a pair of those goatskin breeches, with the hair outward, which are still commonly worn by the peasants of the Roman Campagna. In this garb, they look like antique Satyrs, and in truth, the Spectre of the Catacomb might have represented the last survivor of that vanished race, hiding himself in sepulchral gloom, and mourning over his lost life of woods and streams" (IV,30). Similarly, Donatello's innocent playfulness is emphasised, his pleasure in the dance and simple mirthfulness evoking a gentler Pan and Bacchus by stressing "all the pleasantness of sylvan life, all the genial and happy characteristics of creatures that dwell in woods and fields" (IV,10). But more insistent than these, and more fundamental, is the containment of the subversive idea of the golden age within layers of time, imitation, decay, and death. The first introduction of the faun makes this apparent: "Trees, grass, flowers, woodland streamlets, cattle, deer, and unsophisticated man! The essence of all these was compressed long ago, and still exists, within that discoloured marble surface of the Faun of Praxiteles" (IV,10). This statement parallels the opening paragraph, in which the author notes that the ancient productions of sculpture, the Antinous, the Amazon, the Lycian Apollo, and the Juno all still shine "in the undiminished majesty and beauty of their ideal life, although the marble, that embodies them, is

111

Eve Tempted

yellow with time, and perhaps corroded by the damp
earth in which they lay buried for centuries"
(IV,5). In this description, what are we to note
most, the ideal beauty that remains, or the heavily
stressed decay of the materials? The discoloured
marble surface acts as a reminder that the idea is
doubly entrapped, in stone and then in time: "Ah,
the Faun!" cried Hilda "...I have been looking at
him too long; and now, instead of a beautiful
statue, immortally young, I see only a corroded
and discoloured stone. This change is very apt to
occur in statues" (IV,17).

The golden age itself is offered under an
ironic title, "The Suburban Villa," and dubiously
located temporally "while it was still a doubtful
question betwixt morning and afternoon" (IV,70),
like its original. In the grounds of the Villa
Borghese lies the "soft turf of a beautiful
seclusion" where Donatello finds that he can
breathe freely again, and a scenery "such as arrays
itself in the imagination, when we read the
beautiful old myths, and fancy a brighter sky, a
softer turf, a more picturesque arrangement of
venerable trees, than we find in the rude and
untrained landscapes of the Western world" (IV,71).
Here are numerous mock ruins, "with so exquisite a
touch of artful ruin on them, that they are better
than if really antique" (IV,73). It is a strange
idea, the narrator continues, a needless labour, to
construct artificial ruins in Rome, the "native
soil of Ruin!" (IV,73) But perhaps even these
imitations are old, and "beginning as illusions,
have grown to be venerable in sober earnest"
(IV,73). Thus the golden age is introduced under
the sign of its own falsity, a criticism that is
endorsed by the most damning defect: "The final
charm is bestowed by the Malaria. There is a
piercing, thrilling, delicious kind of regret in
the idea of so much beauty thrown away, or only
enjoyable at its half development, in winter and
early spring, and never to be dwelt amongst, as the
home-scenery of any human being. For if you come
hither in summer, and stray through these glades in
the golden sunset, Fever walks arm in arm with you,
and Death awaits you at the end of the dim vista.
Thus the scene is like Eden in its loveliness;
like Eden too, in the fatal spell that removes it
beyond the scope of man's actual possession"
(IV,73). Beyond the irony and the Victorian frisson
of melacholy and morbidity [3], is a sort of _mise
en abyme_; the gardens recapitulate in miniature the
112

progress of the novel: a cancellation of the golden age, for which is substituted a self-consciousness and a supposedly "higher" awareness of sin and death.

Donatello, the natural man, whose "usual modes of demonstration" are "by the natural language of gesture" (IV,77) [4], is freed from the "ancient dust" and "mouldiness of Rome, the dead atmosphere in which he had wasted so many months, the hard pavements, the smell of ruin and decaying generations" (IV,74); he embraces the tree and kisses the flowers in gestures reminiscent of a lost polymorphous sexuality, before joining Miriam and allowing her a temporary relief from her own troubles. The very exquisiteness of her enjoyment, however, "made her know that it ought to be a forbidden one" (IV, 82), a hint of duplicity in the sources of Miriam's response that is developed further in the idea that "if her soul was apt to lurk in the darkness of a cavern, she could sport madly in the sunshine before the cavern's mouth. Except the freshest mirth of animal spirits, like Donatello's, there is no merriment, no wild exhilaration, comparable to that of melancholy people escaping from the dark region in which it is their custom to keep themselves imprisoned" (IV,83) [5]. The two sport together until it seems a glimpse of Arcadian life or into "the Golden Age, before mankind was burdened with sin and sorrow, and before pleasure had been darkened with those shadows that bring it into high relief, and make it happiness" (IV,84). The significance of this last phrase can hardly be overestimated in interpreting Hawthorne's psychology and his morality, since it opens up a pattern that appears everywhere in his fiction, from "The Maypole of Merrymount" to **The House of the Seven Gables,** offering a rationale for repression, displacement and substitution despite their cost to the individual psyche. Within this rationale even Donatello must be subjected to the higher laws of deferred gratification and intensification through absence: "Writing" or "differance" in Derrida's term [6], appears in the form of "grotesqueness" (discordance, incongruity) as the natural man's equivalent of "art": "In Miriam's motion, freely as she flung herself into the frolic of the hour, there was still an artful beauty; in Donatello's, there was a charm of indescribable grotesqueness hand in hand with grace..." (IV,85). The term "grotesque" originates, appropriately, in reference to the ancient

113

artifacts excavated in Italy; it also registers the
shocking and uncanny aspects of those old objects
[7]. Donatello's grotesqueness, his ancient,
disproportionate, and incongruous aspect, is what
impels him to the murder of Miriam's model and
thereby dooms him to the endless series of
substitutions from which he, if anyone, might have
been immune.

The "Sylvan Dance" itself is subjected to a
critique and finally to annihilation by reference
to the Dance of Death: from the Golden Age "come
back again within the precincts of this sunny
glade" the narrative moves to the qualification
that the sole exception to geniality "was seen in a
countryman of our own, who sneered at the
spectacle" (IV,88), and on to a comparison with a
bas-relief, "where a dance of nymphs, satyrs, or
bacchanals, is twined round the circle of an
antique vase" (IV,88). Then, ominously developing
that Keatsian suggestion, the dance is likened to
"the sculptured scene on the front and sides of a
sarcophagus, where, as often as any other device, a
festive procession mocks the ashes and white bones
that are treasured up within. You might take it for
a marriage-pageant; but, after a while, if you look
attentively at these merry makers, following them
from end to end of the marble coffin, you doubt
whether their gay movement is leading them to a
happy close" (IV,88). A tragic incident is always
"shadowed forth, or thrust sidelong into the
spectacle" (IV,89), which, when once seen, cannot
be ignored [8]. This serves to introduce "a strange
figure that shook its fantastic garments in the
air, and pranced before her on its tiptoes, almost
vying with the agility of Donatello himself. It was
the Model" (IV,89). The immediate result is that
Miriam becomes enveloped by "a strange distance, an
unapproachableness," and the dance vanishes: "Just
an instant before it was Arcadia, and the Golden
Age. The spell being broken, it was now only that
old tract of pleasure-ground, close by the people's
gate of Rome; a tract where the crimes and
calamities of ages, the many battles, blood
recklessly poured out, and deaths of myriads, have
corrupted all the soil, creating an influence that
makes the air deadly to human beings" (IV,90).

As elsewhere, the model here makes his
appearance in a manner that parallels Donatello's:
they are twin shadows of Miriam, neither of whom
can be thrown off, in a relationship that is best
dramatised by the episode at the Fountain of Trevi,
114

when Miriam sees not simply the reflection of her lover, but the shadows of her two familiars: "Three Shadows!" exclaimed Miriam, "Three separate shadows, all so black and heavy that they sink in the water! There they lie on the bottom, as if all three were drowned together. This shadow on my right is Donatello; I know him by his curls, and the turn of his head. My left-hand companion puzzles me; a shapeless mass, as indistinct as the premonition of a calamity! Which of you can it be?" Ah!" (IV,147) Such insistent paralleling – which even includes Donatello's departure after the model's death – suggests that the reader is instructed to connect the two, and infer that the model's relationship with Miriam is similarly sexual. Her obscure remarks to Kenyon in the "Cleopatra" chapter: "My secret is not a pearl," she said, "yet a man might drown himself in plunging after it," or, "It is no precious pearl, as I just now told him; but my dark red carbuncle – red as blood – is too rich a gem to put into a stranger's casket," which are immediately associated with the model ("She went down the stairs, and found her Shadow waiting for her in the street" IV,130), likewise point to a sexual sin committed with him. It is unclear whether the model has a family relationship with Miriam, but it is likely that he is supposed to be either her brother or, as in the Cenci story, her father. The ambiguity of her reference to blood and bloodstains would then perhaps be triple: it might refer to the blood relationship, or to a consequent death – which according to the Cenci hints would be the father's (though not at Miriam's hands, IV,97), or it might include a reference to female sexuality, like the scarlet of the scarlet letter [9].

From this speculative detour we may approach the chapter that follows the destruction of the dance by the model: "Fragmentary Sentences." Here the writer adopts a contorted narrative stance in order to inform the reader of what the reader must – and yet must not – know. To perform this feat the narrator is obliged to pretend (what appears to have been truly Hawthorne's difficulty) an ignorance with respect to the originating device of the fiction, Miriam's past experience. Affected reticence regarding the past is characteristic of Hawthorne's writing: In The Scarlet Letter we are presented with the consequences of an act which is itself absent from the story; in The House of the Seven Gables the original crimes of the Pyncheon's

against the Maules, and Clifford's usurpation by
Judge Pyncheon are similarly projected backwards,
out of the realm of the novel, and Matthew Maule's
conquest of Alice is viewed through the medium of
imaginative recreation in Holgrave's tale. The most
extreme example may be **The Ancestral Footstep**, in
which Hawthorne manifestly had no idea what had
happened to set the story in motion.

The exclusion of what we might call primary,
or essential experience from the fictions is very
striking and results in certain distortions of the
text well described by the title "fragmentary
sentences." Something must be said, but as much in
order not to inform the readers as to enlighten
them. Such a strategy is familiar in the Gothic
novel, from which Hawthorne borrowed many effects.
As Pierre Machery says, "if the [gothic] text is
reproached for futile deviation from its own
meaning, it is also displayed in motion on that
long path which both divides it from and unites it
with its eventual destination" [10]. But the
difference between Hawthorne and other writers of
the mysterious may be seen in a further
investigation of this point. Hawthorne does not
quite belong to the category of writers of whom we
may say, with Machery, "Once the enigma has been
resolved the real meaning leaps out from behind the
screen of all the intermediate episodes. The
artifices of narration are merely the vehicle for a
procrastinated ancecdote." His work rather is
illuminated by that which is not the anecdote, "the
reverse side of the work ...that model through
which it confesses its own nothingness ...this
nothing which – in the interior of the text –
multiples and composes it, leading it along the
path of more than one meaning" [11]. The
occultation of the anecdote behind, or prior to,
the work substantially alters the presumptions of
the gothic or mystery novel, and substitutes
another focus of interest: whereas the traditional
model proceeds backwards from observed effects to
ultimate cause, the Hawthorne variant proceeds from
assumed cause to examined effects. Insofar as the
reader insists on being told the "truth" about the
Cenci parallels, or the supposed faun's ears, "the
book is, to that extent, a failure" (IV,464).
Furthermore, the "real meaning" does not depend
upon the resolution of the enigma, which, in **The
Marble Faun**, is never resolved but remains "clear
as a London fog" even to the narrator (IV,465). It
depends instead upon moralising by the characters
116

Counterfeit Nature

or, more frequently, the narrator himself. The
"nothing" that in Machery's description "multiplies
and composes" the text, in the Hawthornean variant,
is filled by moralised (and sometimes allegorised)
incident. When the narrator finds himself face to
face with the requirements of the reader he
obliterates his own status as knower and relies on
snatches of overheard conversation, or whatever
"Kenyon" is willing to tell him.

In "Fragmentary Sentences," then, the central
mystery is approached and evaded: "there have come
to us but a few vague whisperings of what passed in
Miriam's interview.... In weaving these mystic
utterances into a continuous scene, we undertake a
task resembling, in its perplexity, that of
gathering up and piecing together the fragments of
a letter, which has been torn and scattered to the
winds. Many words of deep significance – many
entire sentences, and those possibly the most
important ones – have flown too far, on the winged
breeze, to be recovered" (IV,92,93). Confessing his
incompetence for the task, the narrator continues,
"If we insert our own conjectural amendments, we
perhaps give a purport utterly at variance with the
true one. Yet, unless we attempt something in this
way, there must remain an unsightly gap, and a lack
of continuity and dependence in our narrative; so
that it would arrive at certain inevitable
catastrophes without due warning of their
imminence" (IV,93). This point of narrative
breakdown might be interpreted in different ways:
as the final neurotic outcome of the formula of
alternative possibilities, as in Yvor Winter's
assault in **Maule's Curse** [12]; as a head-on
encounter with the contradictions of narrative
conventions, as in Machery's observations on the
mystery novel; or as the writer's failure to know
what it was that he wished to suggest, as in
Hawthorne's reported words: "I knew I had some dim
recollection of some crime, but I didn't know what"
[13]. But beyond all these, perhaps, is the idea
of Miriam's crime as an obliterated inscription,
unreadable like the scarlet letter, in the face of
which language itself breaks down. The conversation
is assigned the status of the written (an odd
transposition, since it is a conversation
overheard, for "The wind has blown away whatever
else they may have spoken," IV,97) and it is then
presented as fragmented by tearing and scattering,
which suggests a thorough attempt at obliteration.
It is, thus doubly distanced before its
117

presentation, yet this episode is itself only a discussion with an oblique reference to the suppressed act that unites Miriam and the model.

Their act was contrary to nature: "for I forbear to speak another name, at which these leaves would shiver above our heads"(IV,94); and contrary to religion: "In this man's memory, there was something that made it awful for him to think of prayer..." (IV,95); and it constitutes a fatal entanglement for both: "The threads are twisted into a strong cord, which is dragging us to an evil doom" (IV,95). It leaves, at least metaphorically, a stain on Miriam's white hand as well as on the hands of the model, and "in their words, or in the breath that uttered them, there seemed to be an odour of guilt, and a scent of blood" (IV,97). Finally, in an ambiguous sign resembling Giovanni's crosses like curses in the air (X,124), Miriam contrives to kneel before her tyrant "undetected, though in full sight of all the people" (IV,98). The contours of their evil action are to be perceived only through its effects, the traces that it leaves on behaviour in a city already so full of ancient traces that "one obliterates another; as if Time had crossed and recrossed his own records till they grew illegible" (IV,101). The end of the golden age, signalled by the coming of the model, that is, by the unspeakable secret act, once written but now obliterated, possibly incestuous and perhaps parricidal, is reenacted in the course of the novel by a more presentable version: Donatello's murder of the model, who appears here as the incestuous brother or father.

In his account of Rousseau's **Essay on the Origin of Languages**, Jacques Derrida traces the moment at which, in Rousseau's version, society fully begins, and locates it after the "original festivals" around the fountains. In Rousseau's words, "There at last was the true cradle of nations: from the pure crystal of the fountains flowed the first fires of love" [14]. Derrida comments in an argument which has relevance to Hawthorne's suggestion of an incestous sin: "What follows the festival? The age of the supplement, of articulation, of signs, of representatives. That is the age of the prohibition of incest. Before the festival, there was no incest because there was no prohibition of incest and no society. After the festival there is no more incest because it is forbidden...." Before the festival, according to Rousseau, "Children of the same parents grew up
118

tenderness has taught us to despise the
bountiful and wholesome ministrations of our
true parent. It is only through the medium of
the imagination that we can loosen those iron
fetters, which we call truth and reality, and
make ourselves even partially sensible what
prisoners we are (X,247).

The attempt to return to a state of innocence and
simplicity in "The New Adam and Eve", although
profound enough in conception, falters under its
baggage of assumptions - perhaps necessary in a
short sketch - such as the ability of the pair to
distinguish intuitively between art and nature, or
to use language: convenient but nevertheless
demoralizing paradoxes. In **The Marble Faun** the same
issue is presented with much greater depth and
acknowledgement of its complexity; which is one
reason for the novel's despairing mystification.
       In his discussion of Dontello's lost gift of
speech with the animals, Hawthorne attempts to come
to terms with the paradox of imagining the lost
golden age, for Donatello is able to speak in a
language previous to words, and therefore previous
to the perversions, distortions and crimes
consequent upon the institution of society.
Donatello cannot remember how the chant or charm
was taught him: it is suggested that the sounds
resemble what a boy might make, singing to himself,
and "setting his wordless song to no other or more
definite tune than the play of his own pulses"
(IV,248). In the fountain grove at Monte Beni,
Donatello is almost able to recapture his lost
language: "The sound was of a murmurous character,
soft, attractive, persuasive, friendly. The
sculptor fancied that such might have been the
original voice and utterance of the natural man,
before the sophistication of the human intellect
formed what we now call language. In this broad
dialect - broad as the sympathies of Nature - the
human brother might have spoken to his inarticulate
brotherhood that prowl the woods, or soar upon the
wing and have been intelligible, to such extent as
to win their confidence" (IV,248). Soft treads, and
a whir of wings seem to be audible, and even the
cat-like movement of some small creature, but when
Donatello emerges from his hiding place he sees
only a brown lizard. Hawthorne describes it as "of
the tarantula species" and a "venomous reptile"
(IV,249), reminding the reader of the mutated
lizard with two tails seen just after the murder, a
121

"creature often engendered by the Roman sunshine"
(IV,197) [19]. "Death, death!" sobs Donatello,
"They know it!" (IV,249) Thus the imaginative act
of reconstituting the golden age and its language
of innocence, a language prior to words and
supplementarity, that can communicate directly from
the song of the wordless self to the inarticulate
brotherhood which it thereby establishes [20]: this
imaginative act takes place not when the novel
shows Donatello's innocence, for at that time
nature itself, in the Borghese gardens, was
presented as corrupt; but _after_ Donatello has
fallen into crime, his reenactment of the birth of
society, so that the possibility of a present
golden age has been allowed only under the mark of
impossibility. Either man (represented by
Donatello) is innocent and nature fallen, as in the
"Suburban Villa" chapter; or nature is innocent but
man perverted, as at Monte Beni. The institution of
language partakes of this dislocation, since the
myth of a prelinguistic harmony is closed off in
the very act of its imagining. Language failing,
art (not artifice, as in the "New Adam and Eve"
passage) is interrogated for the clues _it_ may
provide towards reintegration.

The Marble Faun has been used as a guidebook
to the treasures of Italy; it has also been
attacked - especially by Europeans - as a monument
to the philistinism of its author, who felt that
nude figures were an affront, especially if flesh
coloured, and said that although the original
artists had done well to paint their frescoes, the
next great artist who came along would be the one
who painted over their discoloured remains with
whitewash [21]. But all these strictures assume
that the goal of contemplation of art is
appreciation of beauty, which was not true for
Hawthorne; not at least, for the Hawthorne of The
Marble Faun. This novel is concerned with the
claims of art as an imagination of profounder truth
than is available in the observation of the
supposedly real or natural. The passage from "The
New Adam and Eve", quoted above, shows how
thoroughly Hawthorne had already renegotiated the
assumptions of Scottish philosophy, without
embracing the transcendental alternatives. Robert
Lowell's description: "The disturbed eyes rise /
furtive, foiled, dissatisfied / from meditation on
the true / and insignificant" [22], is thoroughly
forestalled by the writer's awareness of the "iron
fetters which we call truth and reality" (X,247).
122

The many estimations of sculptural and pictorial art in **The Marble Faun** bear directly on the issues of the natural and the supplementary, the "essence" and the exterior surface, thus leaving the adequacy of Hawthorne's aesthetic response beside the question. Because of the completeness with which sculpture imitates its subjects, and because of his lasting interest in the point of transformation at which a thing might become vital ("Drowne's Wooden Image," "Feathertop," "The Artist of the Beautiful"); or the living become petrified ("The Man of Adamant," "Ethan Brand"); and parallels between the two ("The Great Stone Face"); Hawthorne thought this art particularly illustrative of the issues involved in attempts to counterfeit nature. Most significant, perhaps, was the permanence and purity of the medium: "A sculptor, indeed, to meet the demands which our preconceptions make upon him, should be even more indispensably a poet than those who deal in measured verse and line. His material, or instrument, which serves him in the stead of shifting and transitory language, is a pure, white, undecaying substance. It ensures immortality to whatever is wrought in it, and therefore makes it a religious obligation to commit no idea to its mighty guardianship, save such as may repay the marble for its faithful care, its incorruptible fidelity, by warming it with an ethereal life" (IV,135). Language is shifting and transitory, despite its pretence to substantiality in "measured verse and line," but the marble used by the sculptor has an inherent integrity which may be violated by improper or irreverent use. As an ultimate version of "trace," the stone is potent to express the highest and the lowest aspiration of the past. There is a contradiction between the cold immortalizing medium, with its endless stasis, and the life that may be represented in it: a contradiction caught in the metaphor of the marble faun, with its potentiality of becoming, in Hilda's words, merely a "corroded and discoloured stone" (IV,17). Such a shift in vision, of course, registers one of the fundamental "transformations" to which the English title of the novel refers [23]. Just as the figures in the Sylvan dance cease to be like a dance of nymphs and satyrs around an antique vase (itself a petrification of the living dance) and come to resemble the festive procession pictures on the front and sides of a sarcopagus, so too does the euphoria of shared crime for Donatello

123

and Miriam become a killing bond between them, like the "evil passion" of Miriam and the Model (IV,93). Much of the novel is absorbed in registering these shifts into rigidity, and establishing their role in the wider historical perspective of society, especially as Rome can be seen as examplary of the history of mankind, and of religion, taking the Roman Catholic Church as a congealed remnant of inspiration, admirably adapted to serve all needs, but become mechanical and even vicious in the course of time. "To do it justice," the narrator comments, "Catholicism is such a miracle of fitness for its own ends, (many of which might seem to be admirable ones,) that it is difficult to imagine it a contrivance of mere men. Its mighty machinery was forged and put together, not on middle earth, but either above or below. If there were but angels to work it, (instead of the very different class of engineers who now manage its cranks and safety-valves,) the system would soon vindicate the dignity and holiness of its origin." (IV, 345).

Hawthorne's interest in the processes by which the living and inspired become the frozen and mechanical, focuses not only on the classic and Renaissance sculptures, but on the contemporary work of American sculptors in Rome, so that work in marble represents both the survival of the past and also the process by which the present becomes past: death-in-life and life-in-death. The American sculptor Kenyon is fully alive to the opposition between marble and what may be represented in it, for he holds, like Lessing, that "Flitting moments - imminent emergencies - imperceptible intervals between two breaths - ought not to be incrusted with the eternal repose of marble; in any sculptural subject, there should be a moral standstill, since there must of necessity be a physical one. Otherwise it is like flinging a block of marble up into the air, and, by some trick or enchantment, causing it to stick there" (IV,16). But his argument is contradicted by his own achievement in the Cleopatra statue which, in the clay model stage, prior to its apotheosis in the indestructible marble, is "fierce, voluptuous, passionate, tender, wicked, terrible, and full of poisonous and rapturous enchantment" (IV,127). The success with which Kenyon has managed to portray the vitality and "womanhood" of Cleopatra inspires Miriam to remind him of the Pygmalion story: "Tell me, did she never try - even while you were

124

creating her - to overcome you with her fury, or
her love? Were you not afraid to touch her, as she
grew more and more towards hot life, beneath your
hand? (IV,127) The "marvellous repose" with which
the statue is endowed (IV,126), is the mask of a
"great, smouldering furnace, deep down in the
woman's heart" (IV,126), but Kenyon is proof
against the Galathea temptation [24] because of his
immitigable decorum or, rather, the insistence of
his supplementarity: all his passion has flowed
into the fetish object of Hilda's hand. "The
sculptor sighed as he put away the treasure of
Hilda's marble hand into the ivory coffer, and
thought how slight was the probability that he
should ever feel, responsive to his own, the tender
clasp of the original. He dared not even kiss the
image that he himself had made; it had assumed its
share of Hilda's remote and shy divinity" (IV,122).
In the marble hand, with its deathlike cold and
hardness, the hand which is "a reminiscence," there
is no contradiction between essence and material
[25].

The "Cleopatra" chapter opens with a comment
on the relationship between sexuality and art which
signals some perturbation, at least to the extent
that it departs from Hawthorne's characterization
of Miriam, who says, quite untypically:

> "Every young sculptor seems to think that he
> must give the world some specimen of
> indecorous womanhood, and call it Eve, Venus,
> a Nymph, or any name that may apologize for a
> lack of decent clothing. I am weary, even more
> than I am ashamed, of seeing such things.
> Now-a-days, people are as good as born in
> their clothes, and there is practically not a
> nude human being in existence. An artist
> therefore - as you must candidly confess -
> cannot sculpture nudity with a pure heart, if
> only because he is compelled to steal guilty
> glimpses at hired models. The marble
> inevitably loses its chastity under such
> circumstances" (IV,123).

Miriam invokes the golden age with its open
sunshine, and (curious terms,) "pure and princely
maidens," in opposition to "Mr Gibson's coloured
Venuses, (stained, I believe, with tobacco juice)"
(IV,123); that is to say, violated in the act of
creation, of the present day. Maidens of earlier
days are, it seems, desexualized by the

everydayness of nudity, whereas the contemporary habits of decency open a space for prurience by forbidding it. Glimpses become guilty (as in Roland Barthes's description of "where the cloth gapes" [26], and marble is attributed chastity only in order to lose it. The substitution of tobacco juice for secretions of fauns and satyrs of the golden age's innocence measures the decline of man, like the "filth" at the foot of the Cross, the "pretence of holiness and the reality of nastiness, each equally omnipresent" in Rome (IV,326). Miriam's attack on indecorous nudes seems strange, given her fiery, magnetic sexuality, yet an appropriateness does emerge if her Cenci-like personal history is considered. The violation of the incest taboo - that taboo which is so deeply the product of socialization as to be reinscribed as natural - was a violation of Beatrice; similarly Miriam's shaping experience must have been exactly on that line between the immediate and the secondary in sexuality. The institution of secondariness in sexual attachment, and psychic investment in images and displacements of the kind seen in Kenyon's worship of the marble hand, creates a powerful cathexis in the making of art objects, especially fully dimensional mimetic images, which is only partially subdued by the coldness, hardness and whiteness of marble and may become dangerously unbound if the statues are coloured [27]. The space opened by discussion of sexuality in nude statuary, and broadened by the examination of Kenyon's dressed but sexually powerful Cleopatra in clay, is almost filled by Miriam's confession of her "red as blood" jewel; almost, but not quite, because the sculptor's own demonstration of his dedicated supplementarity in showing the marble hand, and his unfortunate reference to "brotherly" affection, preclude the direct connection this would entail between them, Miriam draws back, and says, "You are as cold and pitiless as your own marble" (IV,129). The narrator comments, "his reluctance, after all, and whether he were conscious of it or no, resulted from a suspicion that had crept into his heart, and lay there in a dark corner" (IV,129). This suspicion is not specified, but it provides a duplicity and detachment in his response that prevents immediate and honest communion. It is the same reticicence and duplicity of response in Kenyon that is mirrored in the alienations and displacements of artistic technique involved in his sculpture.

126

NOTES

1. All references to **The Marble Faun** are to **The Centenary Edition** of the **Works of Nathaniel Hawthorne** (Columbus: Ohio State University Press, (1968). Vol IV.
2. See the Explanatory Note on page 817 of **The French and Italian Notebooks, Centenary Edition,** Vol XIV (Columbus, Ohio: Ohio State University Press, 1980). A reproduction of the painting may be found in **Art Masterpieces of Florence** (New York: Crescent Books, n.d.)
3. In an uncanny echo of "Rappaccini's Daughter," Hawthorne's own daughter Una almost died of the Roman Fever in 1858, making this passage even more morbid. See Arlin Turner, **Nathaniel Hawthorne: A Biography,** (New York: Oxford University Press, 1980), p. 334.
4. See also IV,77,78: "...he expressed his joy at her nearer and nearer presence by what might be thought an extravagance of gesticulation, but which doubtless was the language of the natural man, though laid aside and forgotten now that words have been feebly substitued in the place of signs and symbols."
5. This heart-as-cavern metaphor may be remembered from "Earth's Holocaust," where it is described as the source of all evil. It also appears in **The American Notebooks** in a famous passage. **Centenary Edition,** Vol VII, **The American Notebooks** (Columbus, Ohio: Ohio State University Press, 1972), p.237.
6. Jacques Derrida, **Writing and Difference** tr Alan Bold (London: Routledge and Kegan Paul, 1978) p.203.
7. Wolfgang Kayser, **The Grotesque in Art and Literature** (1963; Gloucester, Mass: Smith, 1968).
8. See also **The French and Italian Notebooks** on sarcophagi: (**Centenary Edition,** Columbus, Ohio: Ohio State University Press, 1980) Vol XIV, pp. 202,203,213.
9. Miriams "red as blood" secret is later echoed in Hilda's blood spotted dress, just as Hester's "sin" is realised as the scarlet letter, another metonym of the female.
10. Pierre Macherey, **A Theory of Literary Production** (London: Routledge and Kegan Paul, 1978) p.19.

11. Macherey, p.19.

12. Yvor Winters, In Defence of Reason, 1937 (Chicago: Swallow Press, 3rd ed., n.d.) pp.170-172.

13. Quoted in a letter from Henry Bright to Julian Hawthorne, in Julian Hawthorne's Nathaniel Hawthorne and His Wife (Boston, 1884), II, p.236. See also Centenary Edition, IV, xlii.

14. Jacques Derrida, Of Grammatology, tr G. C. Spivak (London: Johns Hopkins University Press, 1976) p. 262. Jean Jacques Rousseau, Essay on the Origin of Languages tr J.H. Moran & A. Gode (New York: Ungar, 1966) p.45.

15. Derrida, Of Grammatology, pp. 263,264; Rousseau, Essay on the Origin of Languages, p.45.

16. Marion Kesselring notes nineteen separate issues of works by Rousseau to Hawthorne. Hawthorne's Reading (Folcroft: Folcroft Press, 1969) p.60.

17. The model is literally thrown into the gulf below the Tarpeian rock, as he father was to be thrown into a chasm in Shelley's The Cenci (1819), Act III,i. Hawthorne describes the chasm as "merely one of the orifices of that pit of blackness that lies beneath us everywhere. The firmest substance is but a thin crust spread over it, with just enough reality to bear up the illusive stage scenery amid which we tread (IV, pp161-163). See also Frederick Crews, The Sins of the Fathers (New York: Oxford University Press, 1966) p. 226, on the model as father figure.

18. Of Grammatology p. 266.

19. Rousseau's Essay also contains the information that tarantulas are moved by music. Hawthorne seems to have known nothing else about them, since he describes this one as a brown lizard.

20. Rousseau's Essay is a probable source of these ideas. See for example page 46: "In a word, in a mild climate with fertile land, it took all the animation of pleasurable feelings to start the people speaking. The first tongues, children of pleasure rather than need, long bore the mark of their father. They lost the seductive tone with the advent of feelings to which they had given birth, when new needs arose among men, forcing each to be mindful only of his own welfare, and to withdraw his heart into himself." Hawthorne also borrowed from the Atheneum James Rush's The Philosophy of the Human Voice (1833), and Charles Davy on The Origin and Progress of Alphabetic Writing (1772); Kesselring, pp.60, 48.

21. For example, see Graham Clark, "To Transform and Transfigure: The Aesthetic Play of Hawthorne's The Marble Faun in A. R. Lee, ed, Nathaniel Hawthorne, New Critical Essays (london: Vision Press, 1982).
22. In Hawthorne, Centenary Essays (Columbus: Ohio State University Press, 1964) pp. 3-4. See also pp. 119-141 on Hawthorne's views on art.
23. Another suggestive title rejected by Hawthorne was Marble and Life: A Romance. See Graham Clarke, in Lee, op cit.
24. Paul de Man has useful discussions of Galathea in Allegories of Reading (New Haven: Yale University Press, 1979), pp. 181, 182.
25. Further discussion of the meaning of the hand will be found in "Footprints in Sand," below.
26. Roland Barthes, Le Plaisir de la Texte tr R. Miller (London: Cape, 1976) p. 9.
27. See the "Introduction" to the Centenary Edition vol IV, lxxx, lxxxi.

In **The Marble Faun** sculpture is distinguished
from the other arts by its several separate stages
of production, one of which is implicated in the
broader economics of the society. First come some
hastily scrawled figures on the whitewash of the
wall. These "are probably the sculptor's earliest
glimpses of ideas that may hereafter be solidified
into imperishable stone, or perhaps may remain as
impalpable as a dream. Next there are a few very
roughly modelled little figures in clay or plaster,
exhibiting the second stage of the Idea as it
advances towards a marble immortality; and then is
seen the exquisitely designed shape of clay, more
interesting than even the final marble, as being
the intimate production of the sculptor himself,
moulded throughout with his loving hands, and
nearest to his imagination and heart. In the
plaister-cast, from this clay-model, the beauty of
the statue strangely disappears, to shine forth
again, with pure, white radiance, in the precious
marble of Carrara" (IV,114,115). Here Hawthorne
stresses, perhaps even exaggerates, all the stages
through which the art object passes, with the
effect of an increasing alienation between the
artist and his final product, and a privileging of
one particular stage, in which the artist is most
intimately involved with the statue. Eventually, in
extreme contrast, the work is not even carried out
by the artist himself but by skilled craftsmen:

"Whatever of illusive representation can be
effected in marble, they are capable of
achieving it, if the object be but before

their eyes. The sculptor has but to present these men with a plaister-cast of his design, and a sufficient block of marble, and tell them that the figure is embedded in the stone, and must be freed from its encumbering superfluities; and, in due time, without the necessity of his touching the work with his own finger, he will see before him the statue that is to make him renowned. His creative power has wrought it with a word. In no other art, surely, does genius find such effective instruments, and so happily relieve itself of the drudgery of actual performance; doing wonderfully nice things, by the hands of other people, when, it may be suspected, they could not always be done by the sculptor's own.... They are not his work, but that of some nameless machine in human shape (IV,115).

Behind the coldness and purity of the marble, then, is a great distance back to the original conception, and the interposition of other hands, making the finished product just that, a product of a series of almost industrial actions by nameless machines in human shape. Against this procedure the narrator posits an aesthetic of sincerity, familiar to any readers in late eighteenth and early nineteenth century theorists of art: the work of art is "true" insofar as it corresponds to the artist's state of mind, it receives its authenticity from the immediate impress of his thought and feeling, like the clay-model, and loses this authenticity insofar as it becomes a mechanical copy [1]. Against this cliche of Romantic and Victorian thought, however, is played off the suggestion that the sculptor tell his craftsmen "that the figure is embedded in the stone, and must be freed from its encumbering superfluities", another touchstone of Romantic aesthetics in which art is naturalized by the claim of inevitability [2]. What should be the divine inspiration of the artist, to intuit the figure in the stone, becomes an instruction to human machines to rid the figure of its encrustations. In Italy, the home of the art most revered by Americans of Hawthorne's generation, the Romantic concepts of inspiration and natural genius were put under some stress by the recognition of the role of craftsmen both in sculpture and in the early schools of painting ("in the manner of..."). But Hawthorne finds the notion of the preexistence of the form too susceptible of moralizing to dispense with it, for after this he writes that "it was impossible not to think that the outer marble was merely an extraneous environment; the human countenance, within its embrace, must have existed there since the limestone ledges of Carrara were first made"; thus suggesting both a natural hieroglyphics within the interior of the landscape, and the doctrine of predestination. "As these busts in the block of marble," thought Miriam, "so does our individual fate exist in the limestone of Time. We fancy that we carve it out; but its ultimate shape is prior to all our action" (IV,116). So the artist's lost intimacy with his own work is compensated by the fulfillment of a greater plan than his, working equally through his inspiration and the craftsman's instructions [3]. Small comfort exists for Miriam in these rocky doctrines, or, for that matter, in the "finely cut features" of Kenyon, which look "as if already marble" (IV,116). The "inspiration" of Romantic theory is transmuted to the severity of a harsh predestinarian dogma, although (perhaps to rehabilitate Kenyon?), the thought is given to Miriam here. A further, slightly recherche attempt to humanise the sculptor for the ensuing scene comes when he emerges to meet Miriam and says, "I will not offer you my hand ... it is grimy with Cleopatra's clay" and is met by the response "No; I will not touch clay; it is earthy and human" (IV,116).

The episode of Kenyon and his Cleopatra (Galathea) contains a suppressed sexuality denied in the marble hand; but which is paralleled late in the novel in his discovery of the beautiful classic Venus which, because of his "love" for the missing Hilda, fails to arouse his full artistic admiration. It seems "to fall asunder again, and become only a heap of worthless fragments" (IV,424). One aspect particularly of his discovery requires contemplation: "protruding from the loose earth, however, Kenyon beheld the fingers of a marble hand; it was still appended to its arm, and a little further search enabled him to find the other" (IV,423). Replaced, the hands automatically take up a position of natural modesty, a gesture which deepens the significance of the marble hand of Hilda's that the sculptor so reverences. What the hand hides is what the hand "stands for"; and it is possible to read the "hands" of "Rappaccinni's Daughter" and "The Birthmark" as similar instances of synechdoche [4]. Marble is the

133

Eve Tempted

extreme example of covering over traces in **The Marble Faun** as it bears mute testimony to an absent passion which still controls the form when freed of its material "clay."

In the broken statue Kenyon confronts the dismembered body of his own desire: it is another version of the passion of Miriam, originally transmuted into the fierce voluptuous Cleopatra which, even in marble, is "fervid to the touch with fiery life" (IV,377), and against which (to placate Hilda?), he contemplates an act of disguished sexual aggression; "I should like to hit poor Cleopatra a bitter blow on her Egyptian nose, with this mallet" (IV,378). His imaginary exorcism performed, Kenyon has yet to encounter the deeper threat of the classic statue, the forgotten beauty of the goddess enshrined in art:

> In a corner of the excavation, lay a small round block of stone, much incrusted with earth that had dried and hardened upon it. So, at least, you would have described this object, until the sculptor lifted it, turning it hither and thither, in his hands, brushed off the clinging soil, and finally placed it on the slender neck of the newly discovered statute. The effect was magical. It immediately lighted up and vivified the whole figure, endowing it with personality, soul, and intelligence. The beautiful Idea at once asserted its immortality, and converted that heap of fragments into a whole, as perfect to the mind, if not to the eye, as when the new marble gleamed with snowy lustre; nor was the impression marred by the earth that still hung upon the exquisitely graceful limbs, and even filled the lovely crevice of the lips. Kenyon cleared it away from between them, and almost deemed himself rewarded with a living smile (IV,424).

After reconstituting this beautiful statue, Kenyon finds it difficult to fix his mind upon it; and the magic departs as "the divine statue seemed to fall asunder again, and become only a heap of worthless fragments" (IV,424). The narrator comments: "He could hardly, we fear, be reckoned a consummate artist, because there was something dearer to him than his art" (IV,424), but the ease and silence of this victory of repression over libido may occasion suspicion that it is incomplete, as Miriam suggests
134

when she asks: "Does it not frighten you a little,
like the apparition of a lovely woman that lived of
old, and has long lain in the grave?" (IV,427)
      The movement from blank and meaningless stone,
into beauty and life, and back again into senseless
material recurs constantly in **The Marble Faun**. It
happens in the revivified Venus and it also occurs
in the figure of the Faun, as we have seen in the
earliest chapters. It is repeated when Kenyon and
Hilda examine his Cleopatra; she responding that
she is "ashamed to tell" him how much she admires
the statue; he maintaining that it has become for
him "a mere lump of senseless stone" (IV,378).
This movement recapitulates the arc of sexual
desire in a rather morbid form, and invites careful
examination of the way in which Miriam may lie
behind both Cleopatra and the broken Venus.
      "What I most marvel at," said Miriam, "is the
womanhood that you have so thoroughly mixed up with
all those seemingly discordant elements. Where did
you get that secret? You never found it in your
gentle Hilda. Yet I recognise its truth" (IV,127).
Kenyon agrees that "it was not in Hilda" whose
"womanhood is of the ethereal type" (IV,128), thus
strongly suggesting to the reader that it must
therefore be from the other woman in the artist's
circle, who has all the features of Cleopatra
(except the Egyptian physiognomy), that he learned
the "secret." And this is the chapter in which
Miriam is drawn (almost) to part with her own
"secret" truth to one who might understand her
(IV,128). She subsides on realizing his lack of
sympathy, and says, "You can do nothing for me,
unless you petrify me into a marble companion for
your Cleopatra there; and I am not of her
sisterhood, I do assure you !" (IV, 129) There is
an ambiguity in this reference: Miriam may mean
that she is not statue-like, that is, subdued; or
that she is not sensuous and passionate, that is,
indecorous or possibly licentious; at least not any
longer. But the denial surely does suggest a
recognition of her own qualities here, if only some
of them.
      The fullest description of Miriam herself also
occurs in the description of another art work, her
own portrait: "there appeared the portrait of a
beautiful woman, such as one sees only two or
three, if even so many, in all a lifetime; so
beautiful, that she seemed to get into your
consciousness and memory, and could never
afterwards be shut out, but haunted your dreams,

for pleasure or for pain; holding your inner realm as a captured territory, though without deigning to make herself at home there." She is very youthful, and has a Jewish aspect, neither roseate nor pale; eyes of a depth that cannot be sounded, and black abundant hair, which is not glossy but is Jewish, "a dark glory such as crowns no Christian maiden's head" (IV,48). What lies behind this? Firstly, perhaps, a structure of sexual alienation: she is beautiful, but dangerous, will haunt for pleasure but also for pain; cannot be shut out of the inner realm, but rules there without assimilation: for "without deigning to make herself at home there" might we not read "without being allowed to make herself at home"? Secondly, Hawthorne's anti-Semitism, as viciously expressed in the gratuitous description of the ghetto: "where thousands of Jews are crowded within a narrow compass, and lead a close, unclean and multitudinous life, resembling that of maggots when they overpopulate a decaying cheese" (IV,388). (Nearby, however, the non-Jewish children have for father the Sun, "and their mother - a heap of Roman mud," which indicates that Hawthorne could be even-handed in his abuse, as is further attested by his remarks about beggars and, of course, Catholicism.) Each of these condemnations is by no means unequivocal, since the anti-Semitism is qualified by admiration for Miriam and for the seven-branched candlestick (IV,371), so that it is unreasonable to argue, as Frederick Crews has, that "Jewishness, earthliness, filth and sexuality are symbolically interchangeable in his imagination" [5]. It is apparent that the fixed point in the chain of signifiers: Venus - Cleopatra - Miriam, is the dangerous eroticim of an untouchable woman, who may, in fact, prove to be based upon that real woman Hawthorne met in London at the Lord Mayor's Dinner in the Mansion House, and described in his notebook and then, in a censored version, in Our Old Home. Tellingly, her introduction is prefaced in his published account by remarks on the relative merits of American and English ladies, in which the American women are criticised for "a certain meagreness," or "scantiness", "paleness of complexion" and "thinness of voice" [6]. These characteristics, however, "only made me resolve the more sturdily to uphold these fair creatures as angels, because I was sometimes driven to a half-acknowledgement that the English ladies, looked at from a lower point of view, were perhaps
136

a little finer animals than they. The advantages of
the latter, if any they could really be said to
have, were all comprised in a few additonal lumps
of clay on their shoulders and other parts of their
figures" (V,334). But in the "Egyptian Hall,"
Hawthorne found a less easily discountable
"womanhood":

> Nearly opposite to me, on the other side of
> the table, sat a young lady in white, who I am
> sorely tempted to describe, but dare not,
> because not only the superminence of her
> beauty, but its peculiar character, would
> cause the sketch to be recognized, however
> rudely it might be drawn. I hardly thought
> that there existed such a woman, outside of a
> picture-frame or the covers of a romance; not
> that I had ever met with her resemblance even
> there, but being so distinct and singular an
> apparition, she seemed likelier to find her
> sisterhood in poetry and picture than in real
> life. Let us turn away from her, lest a touch
> too apt should compel her stately, and cold,
> and soft, and womanly grace, to gleam out upon
> my page, with a strange repulsion and
> unattainableness in the very spell that made
> her so beautiful (V,336,337).

The sexual fantasies aroused by this figure are
projected upon the man next to her (the Lord
Mayor's brother, in fact), who has a hard outline
of face and "monstrous portent of a beard" such
that no mouth could be discovered until he opened
it to speak or put in a morsel of food. "Then
indeed, you suddenly became aware of a cave, hidden
behind the impervious and darksome shrubbery"
(V,337). This gentleman, "familiarly attentive to
her," enables the sexual charge to be admitted,
though only in an anxious jest: "Any child would
have recognised them at a glance. It was Bluebeard
and a new wife, (the loveliest of the series, but
with already a mysterious gloom overshadowing her
fair young brow)" (V,337). The Notebook entry also
identifies this young lady with Rachel and Judith,
like the description of Miriam in **The Marble Faun**
(IV,48), thus ratifying the association between
sexual loveliness and Jewish attributes [7].
        The process of vitalizing and devitalizing the
stone of sculpture repeats the arc of suppressed,
emergent, and resuppressed sexual desire which
Hawthorne introduces always in terms of its

inaccessibility (here presented as Jewishness), but
also uses to explore the experience of life and
death, and as a metaphor for emergent spiritual
consciousness. Hawthorne supposes that the reader
is acquainted with Thorwaldsen's threefold analogy:
"the Clay-model, the Life, the Plaister-Cast, the
Death; and the sculptured Marble, the
Resurrection"; which seems to be attested to by the
"lambent flame of spirit that kindles up
Donatello's features in Kenyon's unfinished bust.
The face gives an impression of a "soul ... being
breathed into him," which may be merely the "chance
result of the bust being just so far shaped out, in
the marble, as the process of moral growth had
advanced, in the original" (IV,380). Kenyon agrees
with Hilda to leave it in that state, propounding
"the riddle of the Soul's growth, taking its first
impulse amid remorse and pain, and struggling
through the incrustations of the senses" (IV,381).
The model emerges from the Catacombs to haunt
Miriam, is killed and returns to the calcifications
of the cemetry of the Capuchins, in which his bones
will be used as stones, like the skeletons of dead
monks made into arches; his fitful embodiment is
reiterated in the trickle of blood that flows from
his dead body in the Church (IV,189), and in the
effect upon her imagination: "as if a strange and
unknown corpse had miraculously, while she was
gazing at it, assumed the likeness of that face, so
terrible henceforth in her remembrance" (IV,190).
Donatello's arc is also incomplete: he is immured
in the prison, but not fully caught in Kenyon's
marble, for that would be blasphemously final in
this structure. This is the area of possibility in
sculpture that seems to interest Hawthorne: the
intimacy of the clay-model, touched by the artist's
hands; the incompleteness that is more suggestive
than the finished product; the "Idea" that
organizes even the fragments of a beautiful statue:
a Romantic aesthetic of the fragment, incompletion
and "sincerity" that also incorporates a moral
perspective regarding the transience of life,
beauty and earthly affairs. But the element that is
incomplete, or fragmentary and suggestive is as
potentially dangerous as sex or crime.

In the aesthetics of painting in **The Marble
Faun** is a comparable anxiety. Inspiration is
privileged over the final product in the sketches
of "An Aesthetic Company" where the rude daubs of
the Old Masters demonstrate the superiority of the
"Idea" over time and the decay of its vehicle:

Very ragged and ill-conditioned they mostly were, yellow with time, and tattered with rough usage; and in their best estate the drawings had been scratched rudely with pen and ink, on coarse paper, or, if drawn with charcoal or a pencil, were now half-rubbed out. You would not anywhere see rougher or homelier things than these. But this hasty rudeness made the sketches only the more valuable; because the artist seemed to have bestirred himself at the pinch of the moment, snatching up whatever material was nearest, so as to seize the first glimpse of an idea that might vanish in the twinkling of an eye. Thus, by the spell of a creased, soiled, and discoloured scrap of paper, you were enabled to steal close to an Old Master, and watch him in the very effervescence of his genius (IV,137).

The charm of these drawings, "lay partly in their imperfection, for this is suggestive, and sets the imagination at work; whereas the finished picture, if a good one, leaves the spectator nothing to do, and, if bad, confuses, stupefies, disenchants, and disheartens him." Ostensibly a stock aesthetic doctrine of the period, Hawthorne's focus here is actually an instance of his overwhelming interest in the idea of trace [8], for the description is merely preliminary to the investigation of one particular scrap, on which, beneath the scrawled pencil marks that cover it, is discernible a slight and almost obliterated outline of Guido's original sketch for the picture of the Archangel Michael setting his foot on the Demon, in the Church of the Capuchin (IV,139). One small difference is that the Demon here scowls at the Archangel, who turns away in disgust; another is that the Demon has the face of Miriam's model (IV,139,140). At the bottom of the well of inspiration, then, is the trace of demonic possession, both a gothic "effect" and suggestive of a suspicion of the sources of art.

Miriam's paintings are powerful examples of expressiveness in art, for they body out her feelings in tableaus of women, "acting the part of a revengeful mischief towards man" (IV,44). Her pictures are of Jael, driving the nail through the temples of Sisera, dashed off as if Miriam were herself Jael; of Judith, holding the head of Holofernes, in almost a parody of Allori's version,

or of Herod's daughter, receiving the head of John the Baptist, and everlasting remorse with it (IV,43,44). The descriptions attempt to neutralize the force of Miriam's work by adopting a humourous tone: "The head of Holofernes, (which, by-the-by, had a pair of twisted moustachios, like those of a certain potentate of the day)," and by instant moralizing : "in one form or another, grotesque, or sternly sad — she failed not to bring out the moral, that woman must strike through her own heart to reach a human life, whatever were the motive that impelled her" (IV,44); but the effect that these paintings have on Donatello is allowed to be definitive. He responds with trouble, fear and disgust, and Miriam admits "They are ugly phantoms that stole out of my mind; not things that I created, but things that haunt me" (IV,45). Yet even in her more conventional, sentimental studies of the winning of love, the stages of wedded affection, or the poetry of an infant's shoe, "productions of a beautiful imagination, dealing with the warm and pure suggestions of a woman's heart"; even these intimations of a "force and variety of imaginative sympathies" contain an expressive trace: a "figure portrayed apart", peeping through the branches of a shrubbery, through a frosted window, or leaning from a chariot "always depicted with an expression of deep sadness" and bearing the traits of Miriam's own face and form (IV,46). Just as Kenyon's statuary bore the ineffaceable traces of his secret life, so Miriam's trouble always emerges, if only in a small figure, set off to the side like a signature, in her paintings. Art is a mirror, in which the uncanny — that which should not have been allowed to be seen but has become visible, according to Schelling — irrupts into the public arena [9]. In **The Marble Faun** art endlessly repeats the hidden faces of its creators and its observers: Miriam and Hilda both appear as the subjects of paintings; and both are seen to resemble the Guido portrait of Beatrice Cenci (IV,48,330; 205,67); Donatello is seen as the marble faun, and is later revealed in his new essence through the idle workings of the clay in Kenyon's hands (IV,272), and the accidental incompleteness of his marble bust (IV,380); Kenyon is revealed through his sculptures and the figure he "discovers" (IV,423,424), and the model appears as the Demon in Guido's sketch for the St Michael (IV,140). Innumerable other instances of "trace" exist in the narrative, in, for example, Miriam's
140

question to Hilda, "Do you see it written in my
face, or painted in my eyes?" she asks (IV,209); or
in the message her eyes contain when Donatello has
the model in his power on the Tarpeian Rock, a
message so clear that Hilda reads it too
(IV,172,210), before the deed "took but that little
time to grave itself in the eternal adamant"
(IV,171). But painting is a special case of that
"engraving" for it is here that the obverse of the
Romantic dictum of "sincerity" has its effect: if
the artist is not sincere, he had better beware the
magic mirror which reveals all that he wishes to
hide.
        "On the emptiness of Picture galleries"
criticises the Italian masters from that point of
view, through Hilda's disillusionment after she
experiences the terror of witnessing a murder
committed by her closest friends. "She saw beauty
less vividly, but felt truth, or the lack of it,
more profoundly. She began to suspect that some, at
least, of her venerated painters, had left an
inevitable hollowness in their works, because, in
the most renowned of them, they essayed to express
to the world what they had not in their own souls.
They deified their light and wandering affections,
and were continually playing off the tremendous
jest ... of offering the features of some venal
beauty to be enshrined in the holiest places"
(IV,338). For "what is deepest" these painters
substituted a keen intellectual perception and a
knack of external arrangement "instead of the live
sympathy and sentiment which should have been their
inspiration" (IV,339). Exceptions to the grand
tradition of passing off a harlot as the Madonna
(Hawthorne's own sleight of hand in The Scarlet
Letter perhaps), are only to be found in the
"humble aspiration" of Fra Angelica (Perugino),
whose Virgin "revealed herself to him in loftier
and sweeter faces of celestial womanhood" than even
Raphael could imagine, or Sodoma who, "beyond a
question, both prayed and wept, while painting his
fresco, at Siena, of Christ bound to a pillar"
(IV,339). It will be seen that Hawthorne had not
escaped from the paradox inherent in his theory of
art: the work must be sincere, but if sincere it is
likely to express too much, the harlot will be
substituted for the Madonna, the secret will
emerge, the statue come to life, the marble lose
its chastity. Only the devout escape, with Sodoma.
The devout; and Hilda.
        Expressive art has the advantage of

authenticity, but what it expresses may be too dangerous to confront: Kenyon is afraid of his statue of Cleopatra, Donatello terrified by what he sees in Miriam's paintings. Hilda's art, copying, has the advantage that it does not reveal the artist but only brings out another facet of the prototype. In part this may be seen as an clash between romantic and classicist aesthetics: as Miriam humourously argues to Kenyon, "There are not - as you will own - more than half-a-dozen positively original statues or groups in the world, and these few are of immemorial antiquity" (IV,124), an accusation which, at least implicitly, extends into the realm of painting and is acknowledged in Hilda's choice to be not "a minor enchantress within a circle of her own" but the "handmaid of those old magicians." Would it have been worth Hilda's while, asks the skeptical narrator, "to relinquish this office for the sake of giving the world a picture or two which it would call original; pretty fancies of snow and moonlight; the counterpart in picture, of so many feminine achievements in literature!" (IV,61) The exclamation mark suggests that there is to be no appeal from this judgement, but Hawthorne's anti-feminist animus should not totally dispel the issue of originality that is at stake. Miriam's originality consists in enthusiastic re-imaginings of traditional subjects; Kenyon too works with stereotypical figures: a certain amount of secondariness is evident even in these examples of the expressive techniques. Authenticity seems to reside in these works only in their guiltiness. Within the deliberately limited frame of this perspective, Hilda's work as a copyist takes on some significance: she feels deeply, and works religiously to recapture the spirit of her old masters, so that "From the dark, chill corner of a gallery - from some curtain chapel in a church, where the light came seldom and aslant - from the prince's carefully guarded cabinet, where not one eye in thousands was permitted to behold it - she brought the wondrous picture into daylight, and gave all its magic splendour for the enjoyment of the world" (IV,60).

The accuracy of Hilda's eye is related to the accuracy of her moral perception: the one sinks into the picture, seeing it fully, and seizing its subtle mystery, even photographing it (IV,67,65), the other probes her friends like a sharp steel sword (IV,66). After her revelation of the evil
142

close at hand, the "gifted simplicity of vision
(IV,335) required for the appreciation of great art
is lost, and she ceases to perform as an artist at
all. But indeed, the possibility of such an
apprehension was always there, contained in the
pictures Hilda chose to allow into her "heart" and,
specifically, in the portrait of Beatrice Cenci.
Day after day Hilda sits before that picture (which
it is forbidden to copy) until it is "photographed"
in her heart (IV,65). But this, of all pictures, is
not innocent, at least not to the voyeuristic eyes
of its nineteenth century admirers:

> The picture represented simply a female head;
> a very youthful, girlish, perfectly beautiful
> face, enveloped in white drapery, from beneath
> which strayed a lock or two of what seemed a
> rich, though hidden luxuriance of auburn hair.
> The eyes were large and brown, and met those
> of the spectator, but evidently with a
> strange, ineffectual effort to escape. There
> was a little redness about the eyelids, very
> slightly indicated, so that you would question
> whether or not the girl had been weeping. The
> whole face was quiet; there was no distortion
> or disturbance of any single feature; nor was
> it easy to see why the expression was not
> cheerful, or why a single touch of the
> artist's pencil should not brighten it into
> joyousness. But, in fact, it was the very
> saddest painting ever painted or conceived; it
> involved an unfathomable depth of sorrow, the
> sense of which came to the observer by a sort
> of intuition. It was sorrow that removed this
> beautiful girl out of the sphere of humanity,
> and set her in a far-off region, the
> remoteness of which - while her face is yet so
> close before us - makes us shiver as at a
> spectre (IV,64).

Nothing in the picture offers the reading which the
story of Beatrice imposes upon it: in fact, the
picture contradicts that story, for, "Who, indeed,
can look at that mouth - with its lips half-apart,
as innocent as a baby's that has been crying - and
not pronounce Beatrice sinless!" (IV, 205) But if
the observer brings to the picture all the appalled
fascination which it is claimed to inspire, why is
the innocent Hilda so absorbed in it? Surely she
participates with narcissistic masochism in the
thrill this painting allows. This is implied also

143

in the scene after the crime, when Hilda sees her
own face and the Beatrice reflected in the same
looking glass, and fancies "that Beatrice's
expression seen aside and vanishing in a moment,
had been depicted in her own face, likewise ..."
(IV,205) The painting's profoundest expression
"eludes a straightforward gaze"; it can only be
caught by side glimpses, or when seen casually,
"even as if the painted face had a life and
consciousness of its own, and, resolving not to
betray its secret of grief or guilt, permitted the
true token to come forth, only when it imagined
itself unseen" (IV,205). The Cenci portrait then,
is an ultimate expression in art of the idea of
essence, it is exactly what it is not, can only be
seen when it is not seen, as the difference of
Melville's description from Hawthorne's attests: he
described it as a portrait of a girl with golden
hair and stressed the "anomaly of so sweetly and
seraphically blonde a being, being double-hooded,
as it were, by the black crape of the two most
horrible crimes (of one of which she is the object
and of the other the agent) possible to civilized
humanity — incest and parricide" [10]. Hilda's
identification with the portrait which antedates
her awareness of the crime of Miriam and Donatello,
and its relation to incest and parricide, suggests
an ambiguity at some very deep level of her
identity which the surface of the text
energetically denies. The choice even of what to
copy may be a revelation in the magic mirror. But
this meaning, it may be more accurate to say is not
Hilda's but imposed upon her from outside, by the
exigencies of construction or, the self-revelation
of its creator who exposes himself in the mirror of
the book.

The problem of originality is, cast another
way, the problem of repetition, the avoidance of
imitation. The Marble Faun is concerned with this
problem in art, the life of the individual, the
life of the species and the history of societies.
Hilda chooses the supplement, thus trying to
circumvent it; by conscious repetition she will
preempt unconscious repetition, become the
handmaiden of Raphael instead of another feminine
scribbler in paint. But the model she chooses is
so full of duplicity as to reintroduce the problem:
in avoiding accidental imitation she enters an
accidental emulation. This is an eddy from the
larger pattern of the novel which touches everyone.
The question proposed by the larger pattern has
144

been called the "fortunate fall": is it better than
Donatello should sin, and thus gain spiritually,
than that he should have remained innocent and
incapable of moral and spiritual development? By
extension, therefore, is it better that mankind
should have "fallen" into experience and the
possibility of spiritual growth, than have remained
in a golden age of innocence and ignorance? Kenyon
and more especially Hilda, have upset readers by
their unwillingness to admit this apparently
reasonable proposition. When Kenyon hears Miriam
ask "Was the crime - in which he and I were wedded
- was it a blessing in that strange disguise? Was
it a means of education, bringing a simple and
imperfect nature to a point of feeling and
intelligence, which it could have reached under no
other discipline?" he replies "You stir up deep and
perilous matter, Miriam... I dare not follow you
into the unfathomable abysses whither you are
tending." Miriam will not be put off, and follows
her question to its logical conclusion. "Was that
very sin - into which Adam precipitated himself and
all his race - was it the destined means by which,
over a long pathway of toil and sorrow, we are to
attain to a higher, brighter, and profounder
happiness than our lost birthright gave? Will not
this idea account for the permitted existence of
sin, as no other theory can." But Kenyon repeats,
"It is too dangerous, Miriam! I cannot follow you!
Mortal man has no right to tread on the ground
where you now set your feet" (IV,434,435). Critics
from Levin to Lewis have delighted in condemning
the reaction of Kenyon and the "hopeful and
happy-natured" Hilda from the secure perspective of
Hawthorne's assumed standpoint. Thus Lewis: "To
the eye of the artist, the color of time was very
much richer than the blankness of the original
sunshine. For such was the nature of man" [11].
Levin, noting Hilda's rejection of the idea of
felix culpa when Kenyon hands it on, says,
"Kenyon's theology is too sophisticated for Hilda.
Life will be simpler for them when they have
married, and returned to the prelapsarian paradise
on the other side of the Atlantic" [12]. But the
question of the "fortunate fall" is deeper than
these easy assumptions allow. Hilda's reaction to
Kenyon's exposition of the theory is not as
laughable as such critics would suppose: "This is
terrible and I could weep for you, if you indeed
believe it. Do not you perceive what a mockery your
creed makes, not only of all religious sentiments,

but of moral law, and how it annuls and obliterates
whatever precepts of heaven are written deepest
within us? You have shocked me beyond words"
(IV,460). Behind the Augustan doctrine is the
gnostic heresy: if the fall was fortunate then the
serpent was the agent of good, and the God of the
garden was evil.

> Since it is the serpent that persuades Adam
> and Eve to taste of the fruit of knowledge and
> thereby to disobey their Creator, it came in a
> whole group of systems to represent the
> "pneumatic" principle from beyond
> counteracting the designs of the Demiurge, and
> thus could become as much a symbol of the
> powers of redemption as the biblical God had
> been degraded to a symbol of cosmic
> oppression ... By Mani's time (third century)
> the gnostic interpretation of the Paradise
> story and Jesus' connection with it had become
> so firmly established that he could simply put
> Jesus in place of the serpent with no mention
> of the latter: "He raised [Adam] up and made
> him eat of the tree of life." What was once a
> conscious boldness of allegory had become
> itself an independent myth that could be used
> without a reference to (and perhaps even a
> memory of) the original model [13].

Hawthorne's awareness of gnostic allegory (and he
read widely in religious sources), would mean that
the doctrine of the fortunate fall was indeed a
dangerous doctrine, provocative of Satanic
inversions and ultimately, as in **The Marble Faun,**
implying an acceptance of incest, parricide and
murder as the origins of good. No wonder that Hilda
calls for silence from Kenyon, and sees the threat
to those precepts which are neccessarily claimed to
be "written deepest within us"; the precepts that
are the naturalised creators of human society. Rome
is itself a "sermon in stones" on the consequences
of abandoning those precepts; there is crime and
blood everywhere and the vision of the city is
nightmarish whether in daylight or darkness. In
daylight, as the opening paragraph of "Hilda's
Tower" describes it, Rome is a "long decaying
corpse, retaining a trace of the noble shape it
was, but with accumulated dust and a fungous growth
overspreading all its more admirable features" (IV,
325); in moonlight it is summed up by the
descriptions of the legend of Curtius and the gulf
146

"beneath us, everywhere" (IV,161). Kenyon, his imagination excited by the idea of the chasm, continues the theme of the crimes of Roman history: "Doubtless too ... all the blood that the Romans shed, whether on battlefields, or in the Coliseum, or on the cross - in whatever public or private murder - ran into this fatal gulf, and formed a mighty subterranean lake of gore, right beneath our feet" (IV,163). These are the consequences of the "fortunate fall."

NOTES

1. M.H. Abrams, **The Mirror and the Lamp**, "Poetic Truth and Sincerity,"(1953; New York: Oxford University Press, 1969); Walter Benjamin, **Illuminations**, "The Work of Art in the Age of Mechanical Reproduction" (London: Collins Fontana, 1973) pp.219-253.
2. As in Shelley's "Defence of Poetry." See Abrams, p.192.
3. John Irwin, **American Hieroglyphics** (New Haven: Yale University Press, 1980) discusses writing in the landscape. But here we should compare Chillingworth's "dark necessity" and "typical illusion."
4. Frederick Crews, **The Sins of the Fathers** (New York: Oxford University Press, 1966) pp. 238,239: says, "with this graceful gesture the statue calls attention to the genital obsession of the whole scene." Lacan would doubtless speak of the absent phallus of the female, but more apposite might be Derrida's hymeneal fable. See **Of Grammatology** tr by G.C. Spivak (Baltimore and London: Johns Hopkins Uniovbersity Press, 1974), pp. lxv, lxvi. See also Sharon Cameron, **The Corporeal Self: Allegories of the Body in Hawthorne and Melville** (Baltimore: Johns Hopkins University Press, 1981).
5. Crews, p. 222.
6. The diminishing strength of American women was a topic of much concern to Americans in Hawthorne's time. The reasons are explored in G.J. Barker-Benfield's **The Horrors of the Half-Known Life** (New York: Harper and Row, 1976), chapter 22, on "The Physical Decline of American Women." pp.256-275.
7. **Our Old Home, The Centenary Edition**, Vol V (Columbus, Ohio: Ohio State Universiy Press, 1970), pp.336,337. **The English Notebooks**, ed. by Randall

Stewart (New York: Russell and Russell, 1962) p. 321. Priscilla is described as Bluebeard's wife by Zenobia in **The Blithedale Romance**: when Zenobia hands on her flower she says, "She is a pretty little thing and will be as soft and gentle a wife as the veriest Bluebeard could desire. Pity that she must fade so soon!" (III,226).

8. See "Footprints in Sand," below.

9. Schelling, quoted by Freud in "Das Unheimliche" (The Uncanny) **Imago** 1919; **The Standard Edition of the Complete Works of Sigmund Freud** tr. James Strachey (London: Hogarth Press, 1955), vol XVII, p.225.

10. **Pierre** (New York: New American Library, 1964), p.393.

11. R.W.B. Lewis, **The American Adam** (Chicago: University of Chicago Press, 1966) p.126.

12. H. Levin, **The Power of Blackness** (New York: Vintage, 1958) p.96.

13. Hans Jonas, **The Gnostic Religion** (Boston: Beacon Press, 1958), p.93.

In Hawthorne's writing any institution of a new order had to be subjected to his constant recognition of the forces ranked against it, often so qualifying even its possibility, as we have seen in **The House of the Seven Gables** and **The Marble Faun**, as to make a virtual satire of its presentation. The greatest opposition to the idea of renewal and regeneration developed out of Hawthorne's sense of the transience and alterity of the present moment, which was always lapsing into the petrification of the past; and had to do so even to be known, so that to know the present was to interpret the marks of its passing. In "Footprints on the Sea-Shore" (1842) there is an early version of this theme: "...it is pleasant, and not unprofitable, to retrace our steps, and recall the whole mood and occupation of the mind during the former passage. Our tracks, being all discernible, will guide us with an observing consciousness through every unconscious wandering of thought and fancy... Thus, by tracking our footprints in the sand, we track our own nature in its wayward course, and steal a glance upon it, when it never dreamed of being so observed" (IX,453,454). The vagaries of thought and fancy are etched into the surface, and readable by the future. But conversely, as the next page of his sketch demonstrates, the subtle record of life, by which it may be more fully known, is itself transient: however deeply the letters of one's name

149

are inscribed in the sand, they will be swept away in an hour or two.

Hawthorne remained obsessed by this borderline between the registration of an action and its effacement, so that his encounters with "trace" are always informed by his insistence upon unreadability: "One huge rock ascends in monumental shape, with a face like a giant's tombstone, on which the veins resemble inscriptions, but in an unknown tongue. We will fancy them the forgotten characters of an antedeluvian race; or else that nature's own hand has here recorded a mystery, which, could I read her language, would make mankind the wiser and the happier. How many a thing has troubled me with that same idea! Pass on, and leave it unexplained" (IX,455) [1]. The question of natural writing ebbed somewhat in significance for Hawthorne, but the idea of inscription of human action grew until it reached the intensity of an idee fixe, signalled in the late romances by the endless repetition of the Bloody Footstep of Smithell's Hall [2].

Those innocently wandering footprints on the sea-shore hardened into a totem figure expressing the weight of the past on the present, as it trod down through the ages, so that the moment of "now," always fleeting, became so superscripted by its origins as hardly to exist. In **The House of the Seven Gables** we are told that old Matthew Maule "trode downward from his own age to a far later one, planting a heavy footstep, all the way, on the conscience of a Pyncheon" (II,20); and given an intimation of the precariousness of the present in relation to the heavy print of the past in this description of Clifford: "With a mysterious and terrible Past, which had annihilated his memory, and a blank Future before him, he had only this visionary and impalpable Now, which, if you once look closely at it, is nothing" (II,149). The triumphant solidity of the past, expressed in the concrete image of the wizard's footstep with its power of annihilating memory, gives the weight of ancestry a superstitious force and the footprint becomes a talismanic trope for the effects of crime.

Even in the innocuous "Footprints on the Sea-Shore" the narrator's assertion of imaginative freedom in the magic spot includes guilty fantasies: "Here can I frame the story of two lovers, and make their shadows live before me, and be mirrored in the tranquil water, as they tread along the sand, leaving no footprints" (IX,459). The implication of sexual guilt subdued within this fantasy is increased by the subsequent sentence: "Here, should I will it, I can summon up a single shade, and be myself her lover. Yes, dreamer, - but your lonely heart will be the colder for such fancies"; and further heightened by the description of three girls on the beach, secretly overlooked as they sit by a rock pool and, "-yes, it is veritably so, laving their snowy feet in the sunny water ... They have not seen me. I must shrink behind this rock and steal away..." (IX,457). Through its association with voyeuristic sexuality the footprint takes its place alongside the emblematic hand, as a locus for guilt and fetishism; with the difference that the footprint registers a trace on the inanimate world, whereas the handprint, more immediately sexual in its pressure, produces a mark upon the flesh, as in "Rappaccini's Daughter" or "The Birthmark."

Eric J. Sundquist explains such moments in Hawthorne's writing by recourse to Freud's essay on The Uncanny, "Das Unheimliche," 1919 [3], arguing that the desire to unveil the secret of the landscape through catching it unawares, both seeing and not seeing, can be understood in terms of Freud's account of the child's perception of a sexual lack in the mother.

> ...perception belongs exactly to the moment when the subject can no longer "see," or see exactly: in a subject partially blinded, perception is itself an interpretation. Seeing belongs to the Eden of simple wonderment in which the child's identity was whole and safe and in which referentiality posed no problem: the narcissistic relationship between child and mother, and between word and thing (image and reality) occurs in a hypothetical realm of perfect mimesis buried in memory. The crisis of perception ... is thus a figure of original sin in that it comprises simultaneously an act of transgression and the threat of punishment meted out for that act. Like the Medusa, which for Freud stands at once for the phallus and its absence ... that which the child perceives fails to correspond with his expectation of identity but at the same time suggests that some thing which was once there to be seen has disappeared; the disappearance is represented by a wound, a mark of transgression. [4]

151

Sundquist's attempt to understand Hawthorne's tracking of nature through the sidelong glance as being linked both to original sin, and (through the castration anxiety), to a hypothetical primal scene is both somewhat reductive and, in the degree to which it insists upon the castration trauma in Hawthorne himself, a matter of unprovable pyschobiography [5]. The trauma is perhaps less onto- than phylo-genetic: the fantasy of the primal scene and the castration trauma are both mythologised versions of a cultural rather than a personal history; more reflections in the psychoanalytical mirror of the sexual relations obtaining within a society than their cause. Along such lines Larzer Ziff argues that "sexually initiated ideas in Hawthorne attain fictive embodiment and resonance as they make sex itself symbolic of other concerns" [6]. This, however, throws the baby out with the bathwater, it devitalises the sexual content by subordinating it to "other concerns," as if sexuality itself were not part of them, and as if Hawthorne's writing did not display obsessive features: the same obsessive features, I would argue, as his society's sexual fixations: "the feminine body, infantile precocity ... the specification of the perverted," as Foucault describes them [7]. Hawthorne displays the landscape as a female body; the scarlet letter is emblematic of a sexual wound; snakes and staffs in his tales have phallic overtones; and the texts are permeated by incest and problematic relationships with father figures; but then Hawthorne's society was similarly preoccupied, seeing table legs as indecent, and feet as fetish objects.

The investigation of seeing and not quite seeing, which always substitutes perception and re-presentation for immediate vision [8], bears directly on Hawthorne's aesthetic practises and the choices he debates in the Prefaces between mimetic and romance treatments of his material. Since presentation is impossible in art (or language), re-presentation, as Sundquist argues, is the vehicle for art and speech. In **The Scarlet Letter** Hawthorne developed the complexities of this idea in language, both spoken and written, and in **The Blithedale Romance** he explored the theatrical dimension [9]. **The Marble Faun** extended the implications of such alienation from "presence" through discussions of pictorial and sculptural art. In **The House of the Seven Gables**, the issue is
152

reintroduced in a form exemplifying the tantalising
possibilities of "trace" that Hawthorne saw so
early and mused upon so frequently: the photograph.
    The daguerrotype appeared to its early
admirers to take its form directly from the object
itself, with the aid only of the sun's rays,
without the interposition of pencil, brush or
chisel; more importantly, without the intervention
of human perception and interpretation. Like the
vision of Lynceus in "The Golden Fleece"
(**Tanglewood Tales**), it seemed to see what could not
be seen by the imperfect perception of the human
eye and mind; not immediately, indeed, because the
process of fixing the image was then so slow, but
without mediation, at least. The image seemed to
peel off from the object, or, as Roland Barthes
later expressed the idea in **Image, Music, Text**
it appeared to be "a message without a code" [10];
in some sense it <u>was</u> the object. Doubtless this is
not quite the case, as Barthes says, the photograph
does have coding; the taking of the image is
staged, the subject and angle chosen by human
intervention; the image is an image of light rays
fixed in chemicals, not the object itself. But to
early observers the photographic image could seem
closer to the thing than any artist's painted
representation of it, and offered therefore two
possibilities: the possibility of evidence,
confirming a particular configuration at a
particular time and place; and the possibility of
deeper knowledge of an object afforded by the
opportunity of fuller contemplation than direct
vision allows.
    Holgrave, in **The House of the Seven Gables**,
uses the daguerrotype process in both ways. His
photograph of the living Judge Pyncheon brings out
his secret character with a truth that "no painter
would ever venture upon, even could he detect it"
(II,91). The likeness was intended to be engraved,
which makes this bringing out of the essential man
as "sly, subtle, hard, imperious, and, withal, cold
as ice" all the more "unfortunate": it is an
impermissible reading, at the juncture of private
self and public accountability (II,92). This trace
is to be suppressed, as the portrait of the Colonel
would have been, had all its features emerged at
once, instead of gradually. When Holgrave intends a
photograph for the purpose of evidence the
correlation between "trace" and guilt becomes even
more marked, underlined by a sort of morbid
inappropriateness. There is a turbulence around
153

this area of the text which is not easy to explain: more seems to be at issue than the diegesis requires, as in the case of the fingerprints in Twain's **Pudd'nhead Wilson** [11]. Why is it, the reader wonders, that Holgrave is so profoundly disturbed by the corpse of Judge Pyncheon while he takes the photograph that may (it does not in fact serve this function) be useful evidence to protect Clifford?

> "Could you but know, Phoebe, how it was with me, the hour before you came!" exclaimed the artist. "A dark, cold, miserable hour! The presence of yonder dead man threw a great black shadow over everything; he made the universe, so far as my perception could reach, a scene of guilt, and of retribution more dreadul than the guilt. The sense of it took away my youth. I never hoped to feel young again! The world looked so strange, wild, evil, hostile; – my past life, so lonesome and dreary; my future, a shapeless gloom, which I must mould into gloomy shapes!" (II,306)

Rather absurdly, Eric Sunquist claims that Holgrave is actually the murderer of the Judge: "We do not know who killed Judge Pyncheon, if indeed he was killed; and though Clifford has been made the villain by some readers, Holgrave remains the most likely candidate" (p.128). But this stretching of a point does suggest another consideration, possibly more significant. There should have been a murder in **The House of the Seven Gables**: the form of the novel requires it, although Hawthorne resisted that direction in order to write a sunnier book than **The Scarlet Letter**; generically, one might say, **The House of the Seven Gables** is an abortive detective story which elaborately reconstructs murderous inclinations and motives, supplies the body (three bodies, in fact, not counting Alice), but stubbornly balks at providing the crime itself. Rumours at the time of the first Pyncheon's death claimed indications of violence: a "print of a bloody hand" on the Colonel's ruff; his disheveled beard; a man seen clambering over the garden fence at the rear of the house. Clifford is imprisoned for the supposed murder of Jaffrey Pyncheon Snr, after his cousin fakes the evidence. Then Holgrave is put in the position of a disreputable detective, discovering the body (without other witnesses); having adequate motives for the crime (and

benefitting financially, as it turns out); and
carefully preserving the evidence required to clear
Clifford (or himself) of the deed. Even the "flight
of the owls," innocently babbling details of their
incriminating knowledge, belongs to the detective
genre that Poe and Dickens were inventing in
Hawthorne's time.

The withholding of the actual deed is
reminiscent of this passage in "Fancy's Showbox"
(1837):

> What is guilt? A stain upon the soul. And it
> is a point of vast interest, whether the soul
> may contract such stains, in all their depth
> and flagrancy, from deeds which may have been
> plotted and resolved upon, but which,
> physically, have never had existence. Must the
> fleshly hand, and visible frame of man, set
> its seal to the evil designs of the soul, in
> order to give them their entire validity
> against the sinner? Or, while none but crimes
> perpetrated are cognisable before an earthly
> tribunal, will guilty thoughts - of which
> guilty deeds are no more than shadows - will
> these bring down the full weight of a
> condemning sentence, in the supreme court of
> eternity? In the solitude of a midnight
> chamber, or in a desert, afar from men, or in
> a church, while the body is kneeling, the soul
> may pollute itself even with those crimes,
> which we are accustomed to deem altogether
> carnal. If this be true, it is a fearful
> truth. (IX,220)

The sketch answers that it is not so, yet even to
ask the question is to demonstrate the exacerbated
condition of the domain of the signifier, in which
the heavenly dagguerrotype of the guilty soul is a
terrifying possibility. When we consider the four
major novels in the light of this we observe that
Hester's crime was merely society's construction of
a "natural" act; Dimmesdale's merely a matter of
omission; Miriam accomplished murder, perhaps, but
indirectly, through the gaze she fixed on
Donatello, whose act reciprocally, was under
hypnotic duress. Hollingsworth did not really kill
Zenobia. And yet these were all acts regarded by
their perpetrators, and narrators, as though they
were fully damning. In The Marble Faun art reveals
the inclinations of its makers; does the photograph
similarly reveal the guilt of one who "takes" it?

155

Of what is it a "trace"? In so far as The House of the Seven Gables stands back from the precipice of guilt encountered in the other novels it does so only because a link has been withheld. Holgrave is very nearly implicated in the Judge's death, but instead of the act we have the photograph. We might compare the photograph to the written trace also: Hawthorne offers a "photograph" of the Judge's body in writing in the chapter "Governor Pyncheon." And the association between the composition of a story and the contemplation of a crime is also made in "Fancy's Showbox": "A scheme of guilt, till it be put in execution, greatly resembles a chain of incidents in a projected tale. The latter, in order to produce a sense of reality in the reader's mind, must be conceived with such proportionate strength by the author as to seem in the glow of fancy, more like truth, past, present, or to come, than purely fiction" (IX,225).

Henry James saw in The House of Seven Gables "an impression of complicated purposes on the author's part, which seem to reach beyond it." The swirl of confused possibilities in the novel would allow us fairly to apply to it Tzvetan Todorov's description of Henry James's own fiction; it creates a "quest for an absent and absolute cause" [12]. All of these possibilities seem to centre upon the notion of clue or trace. Holgrave's activity of capturing all the details of the corpse in the chair makes sense psychologically because he needs to clear himself of guilty intentions: that white, immitigable face he had earlier imagined, apeared then as the face of an oppressor but is now the face of a victim. Perhaps too, the novel needs to clear itself of such vindictive intentions, made only too apparent in its form, as crypto-detective story; and even more apparent in its execution, as Hawthorne calls it, when we consider that concentration on a fly, crawling towards the eye of the dead man. Terence Martin sees this as indicative of the Judge's weakness, unable even to hurt a fly. I think that the implication is more vicious than that [13]. Yet all this baffled ascertaining of clues and traces does not actually clear up the mysteries of the book, it seems more like an ingenious tidying up of the evidence.

The photograph seems to represent a coalescing of the hated Judge into a dead, fixed, thing; a "memorial" valuable to Holgrave. Here the tendency of the photograph is clearly away from immediacy and presence, towards its capacity to entomb the object in a controlled, power-giving, imposition of trace. The Medusa gaze of the camera turns its object to stone in an episode that parallel's Perseus's story in **A Wonder Book**; not the encounter with the Gorgon, however, but the triumphal return with the Gorgon's severed head, which Perseus uses against King Polydectes, who sent him on the suicidal mission but is himself turned to stone by his view of the trophy. This underlying myth expresses the relationship between Holgrave and the Judge: the more so in that Holgrave was commisioned to produce a dagguerrotype for public consumption; it is the Judge's public face that compounds his decease, becoming his death mask; an antidote to the ancestral portrait, a valuable memorial, or reduction to totem object, for Holgrave.

Still, we must ask, what does "trace" signify? Jacques Derrida's discussion of Freud's "Note on the Mystic Writing-Pad" (1925) extends the dimensions of its meaning [14]. The simple device, consisting of a slab of wax, covered by a fine sheet of waxed paper, and over that another sheet of celluloid, provided Freud with the model of mind he had been seeking for a quarter of a century. Writing on the celluloid protective sheet causes the inscriptions to appear on the paper beneath; if the two sheets are lifted the writing disappears, but a permanent trace of what was written is retained on the wax slab, and can be legible in suitable lights. "If we imagine one hand writing on the surface of the Mystic Writing-Pad while another periodically raises its covering sheet from the wax slab, we shall have a concrete representation of the way in which I tried to picture the functioning of the perceptual apparatus of our mind" [15]. Derrida establishes from Freud's argument that difference and supplementarity are conditions even of the original registration of sensations: the repetition of a trace is the condition of its perception; there is no originary presence. "It is a non-origin that is originary" ("Freud and the Scene of Writing," p.203). As the Writing-Pad demonstrates, the erasure of the traces is the necessity of their existence: "Traces thus produce the space of their inscription only by acceding to the period of their erasure. From the beginning, in the 'present' of their first impression, they are constituted by the double force of repetition and erasure, legibility and illegibility" (p.203).

Hawthorne did not have access to the Mystic Writing-Pad, which would doubtless have intrigued

Eve Tempted

him as much as the Diorama, and for almost the same
reasons as it appealed to Freud, its potential as a
model of the mind and experience. In his early
ideas about perception Freud used the model of the
camera, but although this fulfilled one function,
the detailed preservation of the image; it failed
on another count, its incapability of renewal. What
was needed was something like a combination of
footprints on the sand, and the camera: the
features of the Mystic Writing-Pad. And that double
process of writing and erasure controls the
inscription and obliteration of trace as it occurs
in Hawthorne's work. Among the implications of
trace, or trace-making, considered in this way are
the idea of "pathbreaking": the resistance and
breaching involved in the trace's formation, with
implicit connection to the arguments of "Beyond the
Pleasure Principle"; and the significance of
deferral in the constitution of meaning, after "a
mole like progression, after the subterranean toil
of an impression" (p.214). That the preferred model
for perception and memory turns out to be a model
of writing, which is itself dependent upon
deferral, or spacing; and on repression, without
which it is unthinkable (p.216), and which is also
like the lifting of the sheet [censorship] involved
in the Mystic Writing-Pad: all this provides a
point of return to the notions of hieroglyphics,
secret documents, the burning of manuscripts, that
are central to Hawthorne's imagination. Derrida's
conclusion expresses some of the possible
significances of the trace, to which Hawthorne was
uncertainly but compulsively approaching:

> The trace is the erasure of selfhood, of one's
> own presence, and is constituted by the threat
> or anguish of its irremediable disappearance,
> of the disappearance of its disappearance. An
> unerasable trace is not a trace, it is a full
> presence, an immobile and uncorruptible
> substance, a son of God, a sign of parousia
> and not a seed, that is, a mortal germ.
>   This erasure is death itself, and it is
> within its horizon that we must conceive not
> only the "present" but also what Freud
> doubtless believed to be the indelibility of
> certain traces within the unconscious, where
> "nothing ends, nothing happens, nothing is
> forgotten." This erasure of the trace is not
> only an accident that can happen here and
> there, nor is it even the necessary structure

> of a determined censorship threatening a given
> presence; it is the very structure that makes
> possible, as the movement of temporalization
> and pure <u>auto-affection</u>, something that can be
> called repression in general, the original
> synthesis of original representation and
> secondary repression, repression "itself"
> (p.230).

Hawthorne never fully articulated such ideas, and
could not have thought them completely: however
acute he may have been as a psychologist it is
futile to propose him as anticipator of Freud; nor
could he analyse the philosophy of writing as
Derrida does from his post-Saussurean, and
post-Freudian position. Why then this peculiar
consonance between the thought of the trace in
Derrida and Freud, and the imaginative embodiment
(not the formal articulation) of similar ideas in
Hawthorne's texts?

No reader of Derrida can long fail to detect
the nostalgia that underlies his scrupulous
interrogations. To insist upon difference,
deferral, delay and repression is at the same time
to invoke, if only in their denial, hypotheses of
presence, immediacy, fullness: all the lost
integrities of the golden age that was never
possible but has to be thought in order to
establish its impossibility. Derrida thinks these
absences because he is himself a part of western
culture: as he says of his relationship to Freud,
"psychoanalytic theory itself is a collection of
texts belonging to my history and my culture. To
that extent if it marks my reading and the writing
of my interpretation it does so not as a principle
or truth that one could abstract from the textual
system that I inhabit in order to illuminate it
with complete neutrality. In a certain way, I am
<u>within</u> the history of psychoanalysis" [16]. He
writes in resistance to the myth of "presence" but
in a sense, thereby, he belongs within it. But his
examination of Rousseau is no doubt occasioned by
more than careful attention to the history of our
culture's denial or suppression of the written in
favour of the spoken; he is drawn also, for
example, to Rousseau's "incomparable acumen" in the
analysis of speech [17]. Here is a point of
consonance with Hawthorne, who appears to have
steeped himsef in Rousseau's thought, since so much
of what he has to say echoes, as much as
contradicts or qualifies his French mentor. It is

possible also that Hawthorne's relationship with
the American Romantics, the Transcendentalists, is
similar to the relationship between Derrida and
Rousseau or the recent culminations of romantic
thought in Existentialism's concern with
authenticity, another form of "sincerity." Like
Hawthorne, Derrida seems always concerned not to
allow such concepts to pass unchallenged, whatever
their attraction. Both thus engage in a
problematisation and rewriting of the agreed
definitions, oppositions, and collaborations in
suppression involved in their respective cultures;
both rewriting "presence" as difference. The
position each adopts as acerbic commentator is
another parallel; thus Hawthorne's views on
Emersonian vaticism as illustrated earlier might be
compared with Derrida's questioning of Lacan: Of
Poe's "Purloined Letter" Lacan remarks, "...a
letter always arrives at its destination." "It
always might not," is the Derridean response [18].
But of course Hawthorne was no philosopher; the
possible reasons for finding Derrida's work useful
in engaging with Hawthorne are less significant
than whether the conjunction helps to explain
cruxes in Hawthorne's fiction or extends the
implications of his recurrent figuration beyond the
cul-de-sac of psychoanalytical biography.

One of the commonest devices of Hawthorne's
fiction is an identification of a person with a
particular object, which eventually usurps the sef,
or drains its life. Hester's letter and Owen
Warland's butterfly, Priscilla's veil, or that of
the Reverend Hooper, Kenyon's Cleopatra, Eleanore
Rochliffe's mantle, and Holgrave's photograph of
the Judge all share this bloodsucking propensity.
Or a gesture like Sir William Howe's, an expression
like Edward Randolph's portrait, or the shapes
imagined in a mirror by Esther Dudley (in "Legends
of the Province House"), may equally take up this
alterity of life. The tell-tale hardening of the
trace becomes active, stamping its mark back upon
the self: Edward Randolph's expression is seen
again on the dying Hutchinson who disregarded his
precedent; William Howe repeats the spectral
masquer's gesture as he leaves the Province House;
Eleanore Rochliffe's mantle infects her, then the
whole city , with small-pox. Is it the case that
all these magic signifiers mean the same: deferral,
absence, the institution of repression; in other
words, death? If one accepts Derrida's view that
meaning is produced "through the power of
160

'repetition' alone, which inhabits it originarily as its death" (p.213), or "representation is death" (p.227); or if one agrees with Freud the necessity of erasure within the model of the mind-machine, then this may be the implication. The self, displaced out into the world, is then encountered as totem object or mirror image, insisting upon its own otherness, the otherness involved in the origin of perception. Here, "Monsieur du Miroir" (1837) provides a key text.

The appositeness of Freud's study of the uncanny, "Das Unheimliche," has not escaped readers of "Monsieur du Miroir," notably Eric Sundquist, whose very full application of the Freudian idea of the uncanny as representative of infantile or primitive beliefs and animism, and of the double as a projection of the self-censoring conscience, and ultimately as a figure of one's own death, is quite convincing [19]. But if the Freudian reading is not itself interrogated it brings us up against its own form of closure: in which Hawthorne becomes a particularly acute case of neurosis, being filled with ancestral dread, given to associating the home or "heimlicheness" with female genitals; or displaying Freud's transference of the fear of dismemberment into perception itself, as in his Notebook idea of a man standing eyeless, with his eyes on the ground, looking up at him: a version of the castration anxiety [20]. Sundquist recognises that this recuperation is inadequate, for Hawthorne's art is not simply therapeutic: "the act of representation is not nearly so simple" (p.119). Behind the act of representation lies the problem of presentation, of presence.

> Since representation and speculation are so inexorably bound for Hawthorne, mimesis itself nearly becomes a sacrificial threat; his inability to find presence through representation corresponds to a loss of identity that began as a crisis of perception - the very origin, though one that is effaced, of the speculative split between sign and referent that left only a monstrous symbol, the scarlet wound of A. The moment at which A has "real, immediate reference" (a moment present only as fantasy) marks a hypothetical point of transgression - the bloody footstep on the threshold - behind which lies presence, an Adamic state wherein one could simply wonder, free from speculation and the need of

representation: yet the mark itself splinters and disperses that state, leaving Hawthorne to hark back to its point of origin as what can now only be veiled and barely represented (p.119).

This is so near to my own argument that I have quoted at some length: the point being that we require here not simply Freud's idea of a neurotic dispossession of the Edenic state (of infantile or primitive heimlichness) but Derrida's disentangling of the very notions of presence and difference which renegotiate Freud's assumptions. Through Rousseau, some of these ideas were familiar to Hawthorne. Thus the double in "Monsieur du Miroir" is examined not, as might be expected, in terms of his replication of the self, but in terms of his difference from it, not imitator but originator. Hawthorne's strategy is to undo the conventional versions of reflection and postulate the image as an independent, even determining, non-self. Monsieur du Miroir is like Rousseau's description of himself in the Confessions: "There are times when I am so unlike myself that I might be taken for someone else of an entirely opposite character," or, "In me are united two almost irreconcilable characteristics, though in what way I cannot imagine" [21].

The French, or Spanish (X,160), name Miroir establishes a distance between the image and the self, in exactly the same way that M. d'Aubepine translated Hawthorne as the author of "Rappaccini's Daughter." It would not be unreasonable, given Hawthorne's cultural codings, to imagine that the use of such a name holds an implication of license in the double's behaviour. The image does not speak, although its lips move in "visible hieroglyphics"; it simply mimics in silence the expressions of speech, thus focusing again on the gap between sign and referent, the arbitrariness of the sign, the difference between full speech and its shadow. The double is a physical "record" of the author's "heavy youth, which has been wasted in sluggishness, or equally thrown away in toil, that had no wise motive, and has accomplished no good end" (X,168). Through the mirror image, the sketch itself becomes mirror: a device for reflecting the author, whether physically or morally: "I perceive that the tranquil gloom of a disappointed soul has darkened through his countenance, where the blackness of the future seems to mingle with the

162

shadow of his past, giving him the aspect of a
fated man" (X,168). In this way the insistence on
difference becomes a means of expressing identity:
the double's apostrophied independence permits a
self-revelation which might otherwise be withheld.
But the most significant reversal in this staging
of inversion is the attribution of originary power
to the double: "Is it too wild a thought, that my
fate may have assumed this image of myself, and
therefore haunts me with such inevitable
pertinacity, originating every act which it appears
to imitate, while it deludes me by pretending to
share the events, of which it is merely the emblem
and the prophecy? I must banish this idea, or it
will throw too deep an awe round my companion"
(X,168).

The other; the difference; the supplement;
becomes itself the origin; the interiority; the
presence; putting the self in the place of the
reflected image, like the busts in Carrarra
limestone in **The Marble Faun** (but here expressive
of occult fantasy: recalling "William Wilson,"
anticipating "Dorian Gray"), and suggesting how the
predestinarian doctrine which still existed in
Hawthorne's time as the spectre of a too recently
overthrown authority, could become the hidden agent
of dread. We can hardly refuse the implications of
these aspects of the mirror image, which may be
summed up in a phrase of Lacan's: "...the
unconscious is the discourse of the other" [22].
The image represents the future because the key to
the future is discoverable in the unconscious; if
only it could speak in more than "visible
hieroglyphics" [23]. So "the unconscious is that
chapter of my history which is marked by a blank or
occupied by a falsehood: it is the censored
chapter. But the truth can be found again; it is
most often written down elsewhere..." [in movements
of the body, archival documents such as childhood
memories, semantic evolutions (of vocabulary),
traditions or legends of the self] and "in the
traces which are inevitably preserved by the
distortions necessitated by the linking of the
adulterated chapter to the chapters surrounding it"
(Lacan, p.21). Monsieur du Miroir appears
everywhere in grotesque distortions: he is
impervious to time and space, and materialises
everywhere at any time, even "in the heaven of a
young lady's eyes" (X,165). To evade him is
hopeless, it would be like "the hopeless race that
men sometimes run with memory, or their own hearts,
163

or their moral selves which, though burdened with
cares enough to crush an elephant" [the unconscious
never forgets], "will never be one step behind"
(X,169). But what is it that the lumbering elephant
will not forget? The text cannot tell us; it can
only semaphore silently towards the Hawthornean
"legend" which appears in his "hieroglyphics of
hysteria, blazons of phobia, labyrinths of the
Zwangneurose - charms of impotence, enigmas of
inhibition, oracles of anxiety - talking arms of
character, seals of self-punishment, disguises of
perversion..." as Lacan puts it. Or, the legend of
his "heavy youth."

To return to Freud, and to something
previously omitted in the discussion of writing:
"As soon as writing, which entails making liquid
flow out of a tube onto a piece of white paper,
assumes the significance of copulation, or as soon
as walking becomes a symbolic substitute for
treading upon the body of mother earth, both
writing and walking are stopped because they
represent the performance of a forbidden sexual
act" [25]. For Derrida this indicates the problem
of the "archi-trace, not in its essence (it does
not have one), but in terms of valuation and
devaluation. Writing as sweet nourishment or as
excrement, the trace as seed or mortal germ, wealth
or weapon, detritus and/or penis, etc." [26]. And
behind this, of course, the dangerous supplement:
"The supplement that 'cheats' maternal 'nature'
operates as writing, and as writing it is dangerous
to life. The danger is that of the image. Just as
writing opens the crisis of the living speech in
terms of its 'image', its painting or its
representation, so onanism announces the ruin of
vitality in terms of imaginary seductions" [Of
Grammatology, p. 151]. In Rousseau's Confessions is
this account:

> This vice, which shame and timidity find so
> convenient, possesses, besides a great
> attraction for lively imaginations - that of
> being able to dispose of the whole sex as they
> desire, and to make the beauty whch tempts
> them minister to their pleasures, without
> being obliged to obtain its consent" [27].

Derrida notes how this seductive lapse or "scandal"
leads desire away from the good path and guides it
towards its loss or fall. "It thus detroys Nature.
But the scandal of Reason is that nothing seems
164

more natural than this destruction of Nature... Like the sign, it bypasses the presence of the thing and the duration of being" (Of Grammatology, p. 151). For Rousseau it seems a fatal undermining: "...abstinence and enjoyment, pleasure and wisdom, escaped me in equal measure." But the situation is more complicated than that, as Derrida explains:

> The symbolic is the immediate, presence is absence, the nondeferred is deferred, pleasure is the menace of death. But one stroke must still be added to this system, to this strange economy of the supplement. In a certain way, it was already legible. A terrifying menace, the supplement is also the first and surest protection against that very menace... And sexal auto affection, that is auto-affection in general, neither begins nor ends with what one thinks can be circumscribed by the name of masturbation. The supplement has not only the power of <u>procuring</u> an absent presence through its image, procuring it through the proxy of the sign, it holds it at a distance and masters it. For this presence is at the same time desired and feared. The supplement transgresses and at the same time respects the interdict. This is what also permits writing as the supplement of speech; but already also the spoken word as writing in general.... Thus, the supplement is dangerous in that it threatens us with death...." [Of Grammatology, p. 155]

But between Rousseau and Hawthorne there is a gulf - of circumspection as much as years - the Confessions are nowhere matched by Hawthorne's self-revelations, and in the cultural distance between his situation and Rousseau's a large scale shift in sexual attitudes had occurred, part of the movement described by Foucault in his History of Sexuality. The American mid nineteenth century displayed what has been called "masturbation phobia" [28].

The nineteenth century brought sexuality into a sharper focus, paying particular attention to its place in the development of children and, more importantly, codifying that knowledge in handbooks of advice to parents and educators. The dangers of sexual disease and the hereditary transmission of defects took the place of the dangers of "the Pit" of earlier generations, whose religious language could be easily applied to sexual terrors. What came especially under scrutiny in the late eighteenth and early nineteeth century was "the sexuality of children, mad men and women, and criminals; the sensuality of those who did not like the opposite sex; reveries, obsessions, petty manias, or great transports of rage" (Foucault, p.38). The sex of children and adolescents caused great concern to Americans, and especially as it involved masturbation in boys or young men. To those who indulged in the secret vice terrible consequences were promised: at least debility and deterioration, probably death; as we see in this list from John Todd's popular **Student's Manual** (1835):

> 1. Memory is very much debilitated;
> 2. The mind is greatly deteriorated, and foolishly weakened;
> 3. It bears deadly seeds of sickness, and death itself to a debilitated body;
> 4. Everything which pertains to the soul crumbles closer to ruin [29].

The reasoning behind such dreadful warnings appears to have been based upon the belief that the quantity of "vital spirit" possessed by the body is limited, and therefore, since the production of sperm was supposed to levy a contribution from all aspects of the physical organisation, its "spending" was damaging to health. Masturbation was thought to have additional concomittants of listlessness, and the habits of reverie and isolation; that "heavy youth" which would undoubtedly ensure failure in a competitive economy. But hoarded, the sperm would maintain male energies for a crucial period of life, and the boy who did not day dream would have a more effective grasp of reality. Todd's **The Student's Manual** ran into eleven editions within two years, and twenty four by 1854 [30]. It thus provides an illustration of the discourse of sexuality in Hawthorne's period. By these, or similar statements from Ray or Brigham the language of male sexuality was determined [31]. Todd's diatribe against the private sin is pertinent to the recurrence of the "hand," in Hawthorne's writing, and to certain other issues which will become evident after further quotation from **The Student's Manual**:

No light, except that of the ultimate Gods,

can uncover the practise of pouring out by the hand (the vicious act of Onan), in spite of its frequency and constancy. No light can reveal as many modern adolescents as one can imagine, debasing themselves day by day in that way, and doing so over many years. The incitement to this crime, within the power of all, is very great. I have lamented the case of many which, solely from that execrable cause, I have seen come to premature death, some in academic halls, some very quickly after leaving college, and some having graduated with honors. Many are known to defend this practise as if it were some sort of instinct and imperative impulse, and so would have God himself to be the instigator of this debauchery. "This conceals guilt as excuse." Most foul hypocrisy! Those people taught by the light of nature have reproved that crime with many words. "Hand - stay your lasciviousness! Do you think this is nothing? It is a vicious act, believe me! an enormity, how great can scarcely be conceived by your soul; restrain your importunate hand. More than perpetrating an enormity in young boys - it SINS" [32].

Todd promises the resentment and wrath of God, and after the warnings quoted above, 1 to 4, adds this 5th:

5. Punishment by God, who examines you in secret, will certainly come to pass. His eye, always vigilant, observes you. "For assuredly, God himself brings to judgement every deed, including every hidden thing." "And assuredly, to speak truth, they became foul by these deeds." Flee, flee for the sake of life, of soul. "Stand on principles." This is a vice you cannot conquer except by fleeing. Whoever lives in fear of God will teach you "this is the way to the grave," this way leads to the hinterland of death [33].

Perhaps the heavenly dagguerrotype might display even this most secret of actions.

Polemicists like Todd associated masturbation with reverie, but even more significantly, with reading. In fact Todd's warnings came in his chapter, "Reading", which saw the recourse to books as essential and enriching but at the same time a

dangerous stimulus to the solitary mind.
Barker-Benfield points up the closeness of the
connection: "The notion that wrong reading led to
masturbation was coexistent with masturbation
phobia" [34]. It seems likely, then, that much of
the prejudice against fiction in Hawthorne's period
stemmed directly from anxiety about masturbation.
It followed, of course, that wrong <u>writing</u> was even
more pernicious a crime than wrong reading, and
Todd reserved his bitterest venom for the writers
of books which could be misused in this way:

> Some men have been permitted to live and
> employ their powers in writing what will
> continue to pollute and destroy for
> generations after they are gone. The world is
> flooded with such books... And never does the
> spirit of darkness rejoice more, than when a
> gifted mind can prostitute itself, but to
> adorn and conceal a path which is full of
> holes, through which you may drop into the
> chambers of death.

Nor might Hawthorne have felt himself immune to the
charge, since Todd names some rather unexpected
authors in his indictment: "Byron, and Moore, Hume
and Paine, Scott, Bulwer and Cooper," are some of
the writers who have revelled in passion, and
"poured out their living scorn upon their species."
He also makes a connection which bears upon
"trace": describing the dangerous books as
"secreted in the rooms of students" and claiming
that they "leave a stain" which could never be
removed [34].
       There can be little question that the passage
from "Fancy's Show-Box": "What is guilt? A stain
upon the soul ... In the solitude of a midnight
chamber, or in a desert, afar from men, or in a
church, while the body is kneeling, the soul may
pollte itself even with those crimes, which we are
accustomed to deem altogether carnal," deploys the
same discourse of sexuality as John Todd. The
association between writing and guilt made in that
sketch, and later in **The Scarlet Letter**: "What is
he? A writer of story-books!" and the further
ramifications of traces and stains, the making of
erotic pictures, statues or fictional descriptions,
will need no elaboration. But this is not a
question of proposing Hawthorne as one of Todd's
legions of onanists: whatever may have been
Hawthorne's personal history we are dealing here
168

with "Hawthorne", the writer as he appears in (or through) his writing; a fragmented figure with no "real" existence as a man. This fragmented self includes the personal tradition or legend of the "heavy youth," offered within the fiction, but its relation to the historical Hawthorne is always problematic. I say this not to clear Hawthorne of a trivial calumny but to hold the analysis to its legitimate parameters. Hawthorne's discourse is a version of the contemporary discourse of sexuality; his recurrent tropes are determined by the fixations of reference and innuendo of this language. Thus the conflicts between Edenic and artificial "nature", proliferating into the questions of speech versus writing, natural versus human language, and inspiration or imitation in art, all converge at this point of supplementarity: "...that dangerous supplement."

NOTES

1. Compare John Irwin, **American Hieroglyphics** (New Haven: Yale University Press, 1980)
2. E.H. Davidson, **Hawthorne's Last Phase** (New York: Archon Books, 1967), examines this preoccupation, see pp.16,17 & ff.
3. Sigmund Freud, "Das Unheimlich" Imago 1919, **The Standard Edition of the Complete Works of Sigmund Freud,** tr. James Strachey (London: Hograth Press, 1955), Vol XVII.
4. Eric Sundquist, **Home as Found: Authority and Genealogy in Nineteenth Century American Fiction** (Baltimore: Johns Hopkins University Press, 1979) p. 108.
5. The sidelong glance was a favorite notion of American Romantics. See Kent Bales, "Hawthorne and Romantic perspectivism" **Emerson Society Quarterly,** 23, pp. 69-88.
6. Larzer Ziff, **Literary Democracy** (New York: Viking Press, 1981) p. 137.
7. Michel Foucault, **The History of Sexuality** Vol One tr. Robert Hurley (Harmondsworth: Penguin Books, 1981) p. 108.
8. Sundquist uses Thoreau's Edenic longing for a past free from the "network of speculations" in which one could "simply wonder" as a model of this vision. p. 95.
9. There reaching conclusions not unlike those of Rousseau, his mentor in so many areas: "...an

actor on the stage, displaying other sentiments
than his own, saying only what he is made to say,
often representing a chimerical being, annihilates
himself, as it were, and is lost in his hero. And
in this forgetting of the man, if something remains
of him, it is used as the plaything of the
spectators" Letter to d'Alembert (1758; written
while Rousseau was working on La Nouvelle Heloise.
Garnier ed.,p.187).

10. Roland Barthes, Image, Music, Text, tr.
Stephen Heath (London: Fontana, 1977) pp.17,
18;43,44.
11. I have written about this in "Pudd'nhead
Wilson: Neurotic Text," Dutch Quarterly Review,11
(1981/1) pp.22-33.
12. Henry James, Hawthorne, 1879 (Ithaca:
Cornell University Press, 1956) p. 97; Tzvetan
Todorov, The Poetics of Prose, tr. Richard Howard
(Ithaca: Cornell University Press, 1977) p. 175.
13. Terence Martin, Hawthorne (New Haven:
Twayne, 1956) p. 139. I think the point is not that
"now he is so harmless that, literally, he cannot
hurt a fly," but closer to the image in Emily
Dickinson's poem "I Heard a Fly Buzz When I Died,"
or the dead soldier in Stephen Crane's Red Badge of
Courage.
14. Jacques Derrida, Writing and Difference
(London: Routledge and Kegan Paul, 1981) pp.
192-232.
15. Standard Edition of the Complete Works of
Sigmund Freud (London: Hogarth Press, 1955) XIX,
232.
16. Jacques Derrida, Of Grammatology, tr.
Gavatry Spivak (Baltimore: Johns Hopkins University
Press, 1974), pp. 160,161.
17. Derrida, Of Grammatology, p.141.
18. Derrida, Of Grammatology, translator's
preface p.lxv. Lacan's "Seminar on the Purloined
Letter" is in Yale French Studies 48 (1972),
Derrida's rejoinder is in Yale French Studies 52
(1975).
19. Sundquist, pp. 100-102; 113-116.
20. Sundquist, p.112.
21. Rousseau, The Confessions (Harmondsworth:
Penguin Books, 1954) pp.126, 112.
22. Jacques Lacan, The Language of the Self,
tr. Anthony Wilden (Baltimore: Johns Hopkins
University Press, Delta, 1968) p.27.
23. Lacan writes: "What is realized in my
history is not the past definite of what was, since
it is no more, or even the present perfect of what
170

has been in what I am, but the future anterior of
what I shall have been for what I am in the process
of becoming" (**The Language of the Self**, p.63.)
24. Lacan, p.44.
25. Freud, **Standard Edition**, XX, p.90.
26. Derrida, "Freud and the Scene of Writing"
in **Writing and Difference**, tr Alan Bold (London:
Routledge and Kegan Paul, 1978) p. 231.
27. Rousseau, **Confessions**, p. 109.
28. G.J. Barker-Benfield notes that: a
"pervasive and obsessive masturbation phobia in
America took hold during the early nineteenth
century, possibly in the early 1830's..." The
**Horrors of the Half-Known Life: Male Attitudes to
Women and Sexuality in Nineteenth Century America**
(New York: Harper Colophon, 1976)   p.167.
29. Barker-Benfield, p.170.
30. Barker-Benfield, p.136.
31. Todd was actually minister at the
Cogregationalist Church in Pittsfield from
1842-1873. Hawthorne lived six miles away at Lenox
in 1850-1851. Melville's "The Lightning-Rod Man" is
apparently based upon Todd; see Egbert S. Oliver's
explanatory notes to Melville's **Piazza Tales** (New
York: Hendricks House, 1962) pp.238-241. According
to Jay Leyda, Allan Melville acquired a copy of **The
Student's Manual** in 1839. **The Melville Log** (New
York: Gordian Press, 1969), p.908.
32. Barker-Benfield, p.170.
33. Barker-Benfield, p.170.
34. Barker-Benfield, pp. 171,172,173.

BOOKS REFERRED TO IN THE TEXT

ABRAMS, M.H. The Mirror and the Lamp (1953; New York: Oxford University Press, 1969)
ADAMS, ROBERT Nil: Episodes in the Literary Conquest of Void During the Nineteenth Century (New York: Oxford University Press, 1966)

BALES, KENT "Hawthorne and Romantic Perspectivism," Emerson Society Quarterly, 23, pp. 69-88
BARKER-BENFIELD, G.J. The Horrors of the Half-Known Life: Male Attitudes to Women and Sexuality in Nineteenth Century America (New York: Harper Colophon, 1976)
BARTHES, ROLAND La Plaisir du Texte tr. R. Miller (London: Jonathan Cape, 1976)
    Image, Music, Text tr. Stephen Heath (London: Fontana, 1977)
BAYER, JOHN G. "Narrative Techniques and the Oral Tradition in The Scarlet Letter," American Literature 52, no. 2 (May, 1980)
BAYM, NINA The Shape of Hawthorne's Career (London: Cornell University Press, 1976)
BECKER, JOHN F. Hawthorne's Historical Allegory (New York: Kennikat Press, 1971)
BELL, MICHAEL DAVITT The Development of American Romance: The Sacrifice of Relation (Chicago: University of Chicago Press, 1980)
BELL, MILLICENT "The Obliquity of Signs," Massachussets Review (Spring, 1982)
BENJAMIN, WALTER Illuminations (London: Collins Fontana, 1973)
BERSANI, LEO A Future for Astyanax (Boston: Little and Brown, 1976)
BREITWEISER, MITCHELL ROBERT "Cotton Mather's Crazed Wife," Glyph 5 (1979)

Eve Tempted

BRUMM, URSULA American Thought and Religious Typology tr. John Hoaglund (New Brunswick: Rutgers University Press, 1971)

CAMERON, SHARON The Corporeal Self: Allegories of the Body in Hawthorne and Melville (Baltimore: Johns Hopkins University Press, 1981)
CANTWELL, ROBERT Nathaniel Hawthorne, The American Years (New York: Rinehart & Co, 1948)
CELLINI, BENVENUTO Memoirs (London: Bell, 1889)
CLARK, GRAHAM "To Transform and Transfigure: The Aesthetic Play of Hawthorne's The Marble Faun" in A.R. Lee, ed., Nathaniel Hawthorne: New Critical Essays (London, Vision Press, 1982)
CRESCENT BOOKS Art Masterpieces of Florence (New York: Crescent Books, n.d.)
CREWS, FREDERICK The Sins of the Fathers: Hawthorne's Psychological Themes (New York: Oxford University Press, 1966)
CURTI, MERLE "The Great Mr. Locke, America's Philosopher," Huntington Library Bulletin XL (April, 1937) pp. 111-113.

DAVIDSON, EDWARD H. Hawthorne's Last Phase (New York: Archon Books, 1967)
DE MAN, PAUL Allegories of Reading (New Haven: Yale University Press, 1979)
DERRIDA, JACQUES "The Purveyer or Truth" Yale French Studies 52 (1975) pp. 31-113.
    Of Grammatology tr. Gayatri Chakravorty Spivak (Baltimore: Johns Hopkins University Press, 1974)
    Writing and Difference tr. Alan Bass London: Routledge and Kegan Paul, 1981)
DRYDEN, EDGAR Nathaniel Hawthorne: The Poetics of Enchantment (Ithaca: Cornell University Press, 1977)

EMERSON, RALPH WALDO The Collected Works of Ralph Waldo Emerson ed. R.E. Spiller and A.R. Ferguson (Cambridge, Mass: Belknap Press of Harvard University Press, 1971)
    Ralph Waldo Emerson, Selected Prose and Poetry ed. R. L. Cook (New York: Holt, Rinehart and Winston, 1969

FAY, J.W. American Psychology Before William James (New York: Octagon Books, 1966)
FIEDELSON, CHARLES S. Symbolism and American Literature (Chicago: University of Chicago Press, 1953)
FOUCAULT, MICHEL The History of Sexuality (La

Bibliograpy

Volonte de Savoire, 1976); tr. Robert Hurley (Harmonsworth: Penguin Books, 1981)

FREUD, SIGMUND The Complete Psychological Works of Sigmund Freud tr. James Strachey (London: The Hogarth Press, 1955)

FULLER, MARGARET The Memoirs of Margaret Fuller (Boston, 1852)

GREENWOOD, D. "The Heraldic Device in The Scarlet Letter" American Literature 46 (1974-5) pp. 207-210.

HALL, G. STANLEY "On the History of American College Textbooks," American Antiquarian Society (April, 1894) pp.137-174

HALL, L.S. Hawthorne: Critic of Society (1944; Gloucester, Mass: Peter Smith, 1966)

HAWKES, TERENCE Structuralism and Semiotics (London: Methuen and Co, 1977)

HAWTHORNE, JULIAN Nathaniel Hawthorne and His Wife (Boston, 1884)

HAWTHORNE, NATHANIEL The Centenary Edition of the Works of Nathaniel Hawthorne (Columbus, Ohio: Ohio State University Press):

The Scarlet Letter (vol I, 1964)
The House of the Seven Gables (vol II, 1965)
The Blithedale Romance (vol III, 1964)
The Marble Faun (vol IV, 1968)
Our Old Home (vol V, 1970)
The American Notebooks (vol VII, 1980)
The French and Italian Notebooks (vol XIV, 1980)
The English Notebooks of Nathaniel Hawthorne ed. Randall Stewart (New York: Russell and Russell, 1962)
The Love Letters of Nathaniel Hawthorne (Chicago: The Society of the Dofobs, 1907)

HERBERT, T. WALTER Marquesan Encounters: Melville and the Meaning of Civilization (Cambridge, Mass: Harvard University Press, 1980)

HICKOCK, LAURENS P. Rational Psychology (1848; New York: Ivison, 1870)

IRWIN, JOHN T. American Hieroglyphics (New Haven: Yale University Press, 1980)

ISER, WOLFGANG The Act of Reading (London: Routledge and Kegan Paul, 1978)

The Implied Reader (Baltimore: Johns Hopkins University Press, 1974)

"The Reality of Fiction: A Functionalist Approach to Literature," New Literary History 7

(1975-6)

JAMES, HENRY Hawthorne (1879; Ithaca: Cornell University Press, 1956)
JAMES, WILLIAM The Varieties of Religious Experience (Glasgow: Collins Fontana, 1977)
JONAS, HANS The Gnostic Religion (Boston: Beacon Press, 1958)
JUSTUS, JAMES "Hawthorne's Coverdale: Character and Art in The Blithedale Romance" American Literature 47 (1975) pp. 21-36.

KAYSER, WOLFGANG The Grotesque in Art and Literature (1963; Gloucester, Mass: Smith, 1968)
KELLER, KARL "Alephs, Zahirs, and the Triumph of Ambiguity: Typology in Nineteenth Century American Literature," in Earl Miner, ed. Literary Uses of Typology (Princeton: Princeton University Press, 1977)
KESSELRING, MARION L. Hawthorne's Reading, 1828-1850 (Folcroft, Pa: The Folcroft Press, 1969 rpt. of New York Public Library Bulletin 53 (1949)

LACAN, JACQUES "The Seminar on the Purloined Letter" Yale French Studies 48 (1972)
The Language of the Self tr. Anthony Wilden (Baltimore: Johns Hopkins University Press, Delta, 1968)
LEE, A.R. ed. Nathaniel Hawthorne: New Critical Essays (London: Vision Press, 1982)
LESSER, SIMON O. Fiction and the Unconscious (Boston: Harvard University Press, 1957)
LEVIN, HARRY The Power of Blackness (New York: Vintage, 1958)
LEWIS, R.W.B. The American Adam (1955; Chicago: University of Chicago Press, 1966)
LEYDA, JAY The Melville Log (New York: Gordian Press, 1969)

MACHEREY, PIERRE A Theory of Literary Production (London: Routledge and Kegan Paul, 1978)
MCKIERNAN, JOHN T. The Psychology of Nathaniel Hawthorne (Doctoral Dissertation, Pennsylvania State University, 1957, no. 24027)
MARKS, ALFRED A. "Who Killed Judge Pyncheon? The Role of the Imagination in The House of the Seven Gables," PMLA LXXI (June, 1956) pp. 355-369
MARTIN, TERENCE The Instructed Vision (Bloomington, Ind: Indiana University Press, 1961)
Nathaniel Hawthorne (New York: Twayne, 1956)
MELVILLE, HERMAN Pierre (New York: New American

176

Bibliograpy

Library, 1964)
The Piazza Tales (New York: Hendricks House, 1962)
MILLER, PERRY ed. The Transcendentalists (Cambridge, Mass: Harvard University Press, 1971)
The American Transcendentalists: Their Prose and Poetry (New York: Doubleday Anchor, 1957)
MINER, EARL ed. Literary Uses of Typology (Princeton: Princeton University Press, 1977)

NORDHOFF, CHARLES The Communistic Societies of the United States (1875; New York: Hillary House, 1960)
NORMAND, JEAN Nathaniel Hawthorne: An Approach to an Analysis of Artistic Creation (Cleveland: Case Western reserve University Press, 1970)

PECKHAM, MORSE "Towards a Theory of Romanticism" PMLA 66 (1961) pp. 5-23.
POULET, GEORGES "Phenomenology of Reading" New Literary History I (1969-70) pp. 53-68.

ROSS, M.L. "What Happens in Rappaccini's Garden?" American Literature 43 (pp. 336-345
ROUSSEAU, JEAN JACQUES Essay on the Origin of Languages tr. J.H. Moran and A. Gode (New York: Ungar, 1966)
Discourse on the Origin of Inequality (1775; London, Dent, 1955)
The Social Contract and Discourses ed. G.D.H. Cole (London, Dent, 1955)
Julie, ou, La Nouvelle Heloise tr. Judith H. McDowell (London: Pennsylvania State University Press, 1968)
Letter to d'Alembert (1758; Paris: Garnier ed.)
The Confessions (Harmondsworth: Penguin Books, 1954)

SMITH, ALLAN GARDNER The Analysis of Motives (Amsterdam: Rodopi, 1980)
"Discovery in Poe" Delta, no 12 (May, 1981) pp. 1-10.
"Pudd'nhead Wilson: Neurotic Text," Dutch Quarterly Review, 11 (1980/1) pp.22-33.
SUNDQUIST, ERIC J. Home as Found: Authority and Genealogy in Nineteenth Century American Literature (Baltimore: Johns Hopkins University Press, 1979)

TANNER, TONY Adultery in the Novel: Contract and Transgression (Baltimore: Johns Hopkins University Press, 1979)
177

THOREAU, HENRY DAVID Walden (New York: Twayne, 1962)
TODOROV, TZVETAN The Poetics of Prose tr. Richard Howard (Ithaca: Cornell University Press, 1977)
TURNER, ARLIN Nathaniel Hawthorne (New York: Oxford University Press, 1980)
TYLER, ALICE FELT Freedom's Ferment: Phases of American Social History From the Colonial Period to the Outbreak of the Civil War (1944; New York: Harper and Row, 1962)

VON ABELE, RUDOLPH The Death of the Artist: A Study in Hawthorne's Disintegration (The Hague: Nijhoff, 1955)

WINTERS, YVOR In Defense of Reason (1937; Chicago: Swallow Press, 3rd ed., n.d.)

ZIFF, LARZER Literary Democracy (New York: Viking Press, 1981)

Index

Abrams, M.H. 147
Adams, Robert 106
Alcott, Amos Bronson 1,3,6,32

Bales, Kent 169
Barker-Benfield, G.J. 71,106,107,147,166,167,
    168,171
Barthes, Roland 77,90,128,153,170
Bayer, John G. 29
Baym, Nina 90,93,106
Becker, John F. 43
Bell, Michael Davitt 92,106
Bell, Millicent 21,29
Benjamin, Walter 147
Bersani, Leo 59
Breitweiser, Mitchell, R. 28
Brumm, Ursula 12, 28
Bryant, William Cullen 26

Cameron, Sharon 147
Cantwell, Robert 6,43,59,105
Cellini, Benvenuto 39,44
Channing, William Ellery 32
Clark, Graham 128
Cook, R.L. 6
Cooper, James Fenimore 57
Crews, Frederick 4,6,65,68,71,90,106,
    128,136,147
Curti, Merle 6

Davidson, Edward H. 169
Davy, Charles 128
De Man, Paul 43,90,128
Derrida, Jacques 4,6,16,19,20,28,29,73,74,89,
    106,118,127,128,147,157-160,164,165,170
Dryden, Edgar 90

Emerson, Ralph Waldo 2,4,6,17,22,29,32-33,59

Faulkner, William 57
Fay, J.W. 6
Fiedelson, Charles 28
Foucault, Michel 51,52,59,61-63,65-71,96,106,
    165,169
Freud, Sigmund 43,59,148,157-158,161,164,169,171
Fuller, Margaret 3,6

Greenwood, D. 30

Index

Keller, Karl 12,13,27
Kesselring, Marion 28,42,59,128

Lacan, Jacques 73,74,147,160,163,170
Lee, A. R. 176
Lesser, Simon O. 176
Levin, Harry 145,148
Lewis, R.W.B. 59,145,148
Leyda, Jay 171
Longfellow, Henry Wadsworth 22
Lowell, Robert 122
Lukacs, Georges 59

Macherey, Pierre 116,117,127
McKiernan, John 29
Marks, Alfred, A. 71
Martin, Terence 107,170
Melville, Herman 34,75,96
Miller, Perry 42,59
Miner, Earl 28

Nordhoff, Charles 105
Normand, Jean 107

Peabody, Elizabeth 2,32
Peabody, Sophia 2
Peckham, Morse 106
Poe, Edgar Allan 26,75,160
Poulet, Georges 90

Ripley, George 3,6,48,91
Ross, Morton L. 44
Rousseau, Jean Jacques 4,16,17,19,20,28,56,59
     79-82,90,118,119,128,161,164,165,169,170
Rush, James 128

Shelley, Percy Bysshe 6,147
Smith, Allan Gardner 29,42,43,170
Spiller, R.E. 29,59
Stewart, Randall 29
Sundquist, Eric J. 28,59,151,152,161,169

Tanner, Tony 82,90
Thoreau, Henry David 59
Todd, John 166,167,168,171
Todorov, Tzvetan 170
Turner, Arlin 6,105,127
Tyler, Alice Felt 105

Von Abele, Rudolph 43,90,107